DOBRYD

Dobryd

Ann Charney

THE PERMANENT PRESS
Sag Harbor, NY 11963

Library of Congress Cataloging-in-Publication Data

Charney, Ann
    Dobryd / Ann Charney
      p.   cm.
    ISBN 1-877946-66-4
    1. Charney, Ann. 2. Holocaust. Jewish (1939-1945 -- Poland --
Personal narratives. I. Title
    DS 135. P63C483 1996
    940.53' 18 -- dc20   95-8923
                                        CIP

Manufactured in the United States of America

First Edition, January 1996 -- 1400 copies

THE PERMANENT PRESS
Noyac Road
Sag Harbor, NY 11963

DOBRYD

PART ONE

I

BY THE TIME I was five years old I had spent half
my life hidden away in a barn loft.

I had vague memories of the world outside and
I listened to stories people around me told of that
world, but it was hard for me to believe in its existence.
Was there really anything beyond the walls of this
barn? I knew that there were people out there, people
other than my mother, my aunt, my cousin and
another family who shared our hide-out, but it was
hard for me to imagine them.

At certain times, when a German patrol passed
nearby and I was forced to remain still, I would try
very hard to see beyond the walls of our shelter.
Curiosity, doubt and fear coloured my images. Within
their spectrum I recreated the world from which I
was banished. Half invented and half remembered,
it grew in my mind and satisfied the longings that
sometimes came over me.

Yet there was no urgency to my game; I was content
to go on with my life indefinitely.

Some weeks after my fifth birthday, I became aware
that something different was happening nearby. We
began to hear new sounds. The silence inside our

loft was shattered by the regular booming of artillery guns. Planes passed overhead and bombs exploded close enough to shake the walls of the barn.

My aunt, my mother and the other grown-ups became very agitated. Our food supply stopped almost entirely, yet everyone's spirits seemed to rise. The fatigue and listlessness which had reduced us to a state of muteness vanished as we heard the sounds of battle around us. People cried and laughed and talked on and on, as if they had just come together. I moved among them, looking at them with new curiosity, not understanding their words but affected by the contagion of their emotions. I too felt restless, anxious, uncertain. I was waiting for something I couldn't even visualize.

Then one day I was awakened by strange voices just outside the wall where I slept. I sat up, but my mother motioned to me not to speak. The others were awake and listening as well. Were these friendly voices? I couldn't tell. They spoke words that were strange to me. I kept my eyes on the familiar faces of the people around me. These were the only clues I trusted. The voices moved away. Then they came close again. Whoever these people were, they had now entered the barn. They were just beneath us. If they climbed the ladder that led to the loft we would be discovered.

My heart was pounding with fear. The tension of silence seemed unbearable. My mother looked at me and sensed my feelings. She put one arm around me, and with her other hand she held back the scream that was rising within me.

For some moments we remained silent, listening, afraid to stir. Then I saw my cousin Alexander move cautiously to the edge of the loft. I held my breath as he leaned over the edge. When he turned back to us I saw that he was smiling. I heard him whisper to the others: "It's all right. They're Russians. I'm sure of it." Still no one moved. The habits of long months of hiding could not be abandoned without an effort. We waited.

Then someone began to sing. It was a song I knew. One of the Russian refugees in our loft, a man whom I called Uncle Joseph, had taught it to me. At first I thought that it was he who was singing. I turned to look at him and I saw that his lips were not moving. Then I realized that the voice was a woman's and that it came from below us. I became very excited. Again I looked to the others to see what it meant, and I saw that they were crying. My confusion increased.

When the song was over, a man spoke in Polish: "We are your friends. There are Jews amongst us. Trust us." He repeated these words again slowly.

My cousin returned to the edge of the loft and leaned down. "We are up here. There are seven of us and a child. Please help us to come down."

Then it seemed to me as if everyone around me went mad. My mother no longer covered my mouth with her hand, but in any case I had become mute. I looked at the people I knew so well and they seemed almost strangers in their behaviour. Weeping and laughing at the same time, they hugged me and embraced one another. I felt smothered in their arms. These embraces were not the ones I was used to; too tight, too close. I was frightened.

A young man appeared at the top of the ladder. I saw him pick up my aunt and carry her down. I had to see what he was doing to her. I crept closer to the edge. Below me I saw other soldiers, men and women in uniform, with rifles in their arms. My aunt and the young man reached the ground and they sat down in the straw. He continued to hold my aunt and I saw him rock her gently as my mother rocked me sometimes.

I wanted to go to my aunt and comfort her. But I had forgotten that for the last few days I had been too weak to stand. Now as I tried to rise, my legs folded beneath me and the walls of the barn seemed to tilt away from the ground.

Someone, another stranger, his arms stronger than those that usually held me, picked me up and carried me down the ladder. We stopped near the doorway. I could see past his shoulder. For the first time that I could remember I looked out and into the forbidden world.

A large orange circle covered the sky and coloured the world below. The fields, the animals, the farmhouse, all were illuminated in this strange, intense, blood-like colour. Suddenly I felt terrified in a way that was worse than all my previous experiences of fear. I heard myself scream, again and again. I couldn't stop. At the same time my body went rigid with the effort of trying to get away from the doorway.

I was certain we were in a trap. The enemy I had so often been warned about had tricked everyone around me. My mother was trapped in the arms of a stranger. My aunt sat peacefully close to another, her long hair spread trustingly over his arm. I would not be fooled like this. I would rather die than leave the barn to step into the horror outside. My past fears of bombs, probing bayonets and tracking dogs were nothing compared to the terror I now felt. I would never leave. Never.

The scream that I had kept inside me for so long

continued to pour forth. Everyone stopped. A look of familiar fear returned to their faces. They rushed over to stifle my noise. For them I was still a source of danger in their midst, the most vulnerable point in their defence. In the past they had doubted my mother's reassurances. Now a hand came over my mouth, and my arms and legs were held as I continued to struggle.

The soldier who held me managed to calm them. I was extricated from those desperate arms and carried over to a corner away from the doorway. My new protector soothed me with his gentle voice. He spoke Russian, and I could only understand a little of what he said, but it felt good to listen to him and be near him. I was fascinated by his appearance— so different from the hollowed faces that I knew reflected my own.

We stayed inside for some hours, waiting for a vehicle to be brought around to move us. During this time the soldiers shared some of their bread with us. One of them took out a harmonica. While he played, his friends sang. Once again I saw that people were crying, but their faces had a new expression. I began to understand that there were many different reasons for tears.

It was evening when the carriages arrived. Outside the barn the world now appeared a soft blue colour. My new friend, whose name I had learned was Yuri, picked me up and carried me outside. All the while his soft voice reassured me, and the sound of those words made me feel safe. They also bound me to him forever.

The fresh air of the summer evening felt soothing against my skin. I looked around me. I was no longer afraid.

II

WE CAME OUT of the loft at the end of summer, near harvest time. Even in the midst of war the farmers continued to work their fields. The air was filled with the fragrance of ripe grain. We saw very little of what we passed. When we left our hiding place for the last time it was nearly night. Soon we were travelling in darkness.

Our carriage moved slowly through the open countryside. I sensed, without seeing, the vast empty stretches of space. Shrouded by obscurity, I felt myself overwhelmed by new sensations. The night yielded many clues and I grasped at them eagerly, straining to see into the darkness. The walls of the barn had fallen away, but the outside world continued to elude me.

A gentle wind touched my skin, my hair, with new, delicious sensations. The odours that reached me reminded me of my past fantasies about the world unknown to me. As we drove through the night I saw the shapes of farmhouses outlined in the dark. Here and there in a distant house a light could be seen. Once, we passed a group of people returning from the fields. Suddenly I was glad of the darkness that hid our misery from strangers' eyes.

We were travelling in a horse-drawn cart. Behind us followed another filled with the soldiers who had liberated us. The two carriages were in such sharp contrast that they might have served as an allegoric illustration of life and death.

In ours, everyone lay drained and silent. Throughout the night's ride we were often closer to the dead
than to the world of the living we had just re-entered.
Memories of those who were not with us surrounded
us. Even as I sat pressed close to my mother, I knew
that her thoughts were far away, perhaps with my
father, whom she hadn't seen in three years.

I had only just realized that not all people looked
like the ones I had known in the loft. The sight of
our vigorous liberators had reawakened us to the sad
state of our own physical condition. In the loft we
had forgotten the normal world and its appearance,
and had become detached from our past lives. Now
we could see for the first time how far we had been
removed. We looked at one another outside the loft
with different eyes, and we shrank from each other
with a new sense of shame.

Our ride was silent. Behind us followed the other
carriage, and from it flowed a constant stream of noise
and celebration. Occasionally one of the soldiers
would jump down and come over to see how we were
doing. For a moment a spark of animation would
go through us. Then his friends would call him back
and he would return to join in a song, or catch the
last line of a story that would produce a new outburst
of laughter.

I listened to these sounds with a sense of wonder.
The mood of the people whose bodies touched mine
had no hold on me. I was immune to it by right of
childhood. I wanted to be with the others. It seemed
to me that I belonged to them. Given the choice, I
would have quickly abandoned the arms that held
me, the quiet sighs, the smell of confinement and illness, and gone off to join the others.

I listened to their strong voices, their songs, and

even at this distance from them I was happy. Happy for the first time in a way that was not related to the satisfaction of some physical need, such as being momentarily full or warm. This was a different sensation, vague, not localized, yet intense. I was surprised to find that it brought tears to my eyes. My mother, misunderstanding, roused herself to comfort me. I accepted her endearments passively and for the first time I felt distant from her. My attention was focused on the new, strange feelings inside of me. I hardly heard her.

The ride seemed to last all night. I fell asleep several times and each time I awoke I wished the trip would never end. I wanted to hold on forever to the sensations roused by this new experience, to the night air that surrounded me. Between these two forces I felt myself floating light and free.

Again I fell asleep and when I opened my eyes I saw that we were in a village. The houses were dark, closed up for the night, and the streets were deserted.

We stopped in front of a farmhouse near the outskirts of the village. The soldiers knocked on the shutters with their rifles and finally a light went on inside. The door was opened by an old man. He lifted his lantern to get a better look at this strange procession that had arrived at his house in the middle of the night.

One of the soldiers called to him: "Over here, old man. Give us a hand. We've brought you some guests."

He came closer. Now his light shone into our cart. He stared at us, his eyes wide with horror. "Dear God," I heard him whisper, and his free hand went up to make the sign of the cross.

"What are you scared of, you old fool?" the soldiers teased him. "They're people just like you and me.

You take good care of them for a few days and you'll
see how well they'll look. Now come on, give us a
hand."

The farmer stumbled backwards seeking a way out.
The soldiers raised their guns and he turned to follow
them.

Three of the survivors were carried inside. When
they were settled, one of the soldiers stayed behind
to guard them, and our cart moved on.

Soon we stopped in front of another farmhouse.
Two soldiers gave their orders and we waited while
the people inside prepared our beds. Yuri, my friend,
came over to us. He lifted me out and sat me down
in the grass. Then he turned towards the old woman
whom I had been taught to call Grandmother during
the months in the loft. She lay motionless in his arms,
as she had been throughout the ride. Yuri looked
at her closely. It was hard to see anything in the dark.
He called to his friend who came over with a flashlight.
They shone it on her face. I could see that her eyes
were open, yet she looked as if she were asleep. Before
the light went out I saw the soldier close her eyes
and put her back into the wagon.

I was too tired to question them. I felt myself carried
inside and put to bed. I fell asleep, warm and comfortable. I was in a real bed for the first time that I could
remember. For a moment I thought of Grandmother,
and I wondered why they had left her outside alone
in the cart. I decided I would wait till morning to
ask my mother about it.

The next day there was no sign of Grandmother,
and I forgot all about her. New experiences and
pleasures closed out everything else. Yesterday's

events were already part of a half-remembered nightmare.

III

IT WAS DECIDED that we would remain in the village
until the Russians were ready to advance.

The Germans were retreating. Small bands of them,
cut off from the main line of retreat, still roamed
the countryside making the roads impassable and dangerous. Alone, we would never make it back to our
home in Dobryd. After such a long absence, my
mother and my aunt resigned themselves to waiting
out the last few weeks of war a few kilometres from
their home.

My cousin Alexander was no longer with us. This
was the only painful event that I experienced during
the first weeks of freedom. As soon as he had recovered his strength he decided to join a local band of
partisans and fight the Germans. My aunt and my
mother pleaded with him not to go. The war was
almost over. The Germans were already defeated.
Why should he now risk the life that they had saved
against such odds?

Alex heard them out, but there was nothing they
could say to change his mind. He had always wanted
to fight. He had remained in the loft only because
of our need for him.

Now that we were free and protected he could at
last do what he had so often talked about. He was
eighteen, burning with the need for revenge, and so

he left us. We missed him terribly. Yet so much was happening to me during those first weeks of freedom that I was never sad for long. I had no idea that he was in danger and so it was easy to think of other things.

War still raged around us, but miraculously the village that sheltered us remained untouched and seemingly unconcerned. We awoke each morning to the crowing of roosters and the distant firing of artillery shells. The peasants went through their morning chores. The animals waited to be fed. The repetitive pattern of farm life continued, unaltered from one day to the next, as it had from generation to generation, so that it had acquired the permanence of nature itself.

Danger seemed unlikely in this setting. Each day I felt safer and more secure. After a while it seemed to me that my own life was part of the peaceful, rooted existence of the village. I discarded the past as eagerly as I took to my new life.

Now the outside world was within reach. The room I slept in, the yard out front, the neighbouring houses, the trees, the animals and the sky were all unquestionably real. I began to think of my months in the loft as a story that had happened to someone else. Everything in me turned towards the new world, the real world, as a plant bends towards the sun.

I suppose the world in which I found shelter did not really exist, at least not in the way that I perceived it.

These same peasants who under Russian orders fed us from supplies hoarded with the reflex of their forefathers, who fussed over us with home remedies and peasant potions, would have considered it a fine amusement two months earlier to turn us over to the Germans and watch our execution. Our presence among them was only another load in an already burdened existence. They sheltered us when they had to, or if it were profitable. Otherwise they would turn us out with no remorse. Centuries of occupation and maltreatment had developed in them the capacity for flexible neutrality; they satisfied their masters, whoever they might be, and at the same time they continued to survive and to outlast them.

I had no suspicion of this at the time. While my mother and my aunt remained unmoved by the reverence and attention which they received from our hosts, I was completely won over. I liked the old couple, Djunek and Marisia, but most of all I liked their daughter, Kazia. They, of course, realized what a natural ally they had in me and made the most of it. They fussed over me, exaggerated my qualities, showered me with endearments, and I repaid them with utter devotion. My family's attempts at restraint were hopeless. With a child's typical hedonism in the face of pleasure I would not allow any criticism of my new friends.

One day Kazia called me into her room. "I have a surprise for you," she said. As I held back, considering for a moment whether the word surprise meant something pleasant or unpleasant, Kazia came over and picked me up. We went into her room. I noticed a photograph of her husband, in uniform, smiling at us. She put me down on the bed, piled so high with quilts that I sank into it as into deep water.

She got down on her knees and pulled out a box from beneath the bed. I took it from her and looked inside. There was a doll that Kazia had made from bits of cloth and stuffed with straw. She had two braids, as I did, and a cheerful smile had been embroidered on her face.

"Do you like it? Take it. I made it for you. It's yours to keep. Forever. There's only one thing you have to do. You must promise to tell Kazia everything that she asks you." I promised eagerly.

"All right. Did you ever see your mother or your aunt putting anything in the ground? Think hard for a moment. This is very important."

I did as Kazia told me, but there was nothing for me to remember. I shook my head.

"Did you ever hear them talk of hiding anything? No? But it's not possible. They must have put it somewhere. You see little one, I know who your grandfather was. His estate was not too far from this village. He and his family must have buried all kinds of treasures. Try again. Promise me if it ever comes to you, you'll come right away and tell me. Kazia will be very good to you. I'll make more dolls and I'll make you pretty clothes for them."

At that moment I still loved Kazia. I would have done anything to please her, without a second thought for my mother's warnings. But I had never heard of any buried treasure. There was nothing I could tell.

She finally released me, with my new doll, and I never mentioned the incident to my mother. From then on, however, I was uncomfortable in her presence. I was afraid that she might press me again for information, and still I would have nothing to tell her. I dreaded the thought of disappointing her and from then on I tried to avoid being alone with Kazia.

IV

MY DAYS IN the village were so different from what had preceded them that it often seemed to me as if my real life began at the moment of liberation. It pleased me to think I had been born into the world at the age of five in this farmhouse. Like the newborn, I was quick to forget my previous existence.

The first few days were very simple and alike. I was too weak to do more than rest and eat and sleep. But even then, at the very beginning, each new day began as a strange adventure in discovery. Every morning, as I lay under a light eiderdown cover, surrounded by unfamiliar sounds and odours, I gave myself over to the pleasures of anticipation. Everything seemed possible in those moments, and I was content to let the waiting go on forever. The mood of those mornings set a pattern for the future: in the years to come the feeling of anticipation became more pleasurable for me than its realization.

My first explorations began with food. The taste of food alone, food other than the bread or potatoes that had kept me alive in the loft, provided me with more stimulus than I could cope with at the start.

The first morning, Marisia, the old woman, brought me some fresh milk fortified by a raw egg. The mixture looked strange to me, and the odour made me feel faint, but I was so eager to begin my new life that I gulped it down quickly. The result was disastrous. Suddenly I was ill and vomiting, and it took hours for the attack to subside.

The violence of this beginning frightened the adults. As I lay weak and dizzy I heard them whispering about me. It was decided that I would have to be introduced to food as slowly as a baby. But I had no time for such procedures. I was impatient and greedy. Not so much for food itself but for what it represented to me—the richness and variety of my new life. I was propelled towards it by a powerful force that was set in motion the first time I stepped outside the world of the barn.

With food, there was soon the added pleasure of being able to stand upright. In our hiding place I had spent most of my time lying down or sitting. Our little loft was not very high and the eight of us, when we stretched out, filled it completely. Most of the time we had also been too weak to move around. Now I discovered the freedom of having space to move in.

The idea of endless space fascinated me. At first the main room of the house, where I remained most of the day, seemed to me infinite. Often, I explored its vastness with my eyes closed. Whenever my mother caught me doing this she became very annoyed with me. I could not make her understand the pleasure I found in the extended distances I created for myself by coming upon physical limits unexpectedly.

Once the interior became familiar and finite I ventured outside. At first it frightened me to go out of the house. Somehow it seemed to me a shameful exposure. But my desire to continue this adventure proved to be stronger than my timidity. My mother warned me not to wander away. I had to remain within sight of the house, but this did not restrict my pleasure.

In any case, I don't think I would have dared to go farther than the familiar landmarks of the farmyard.

When the weather was fine I stayed outside as much as I could. I was alone most of the time. The villagers avoided us through superstition. They had not yet made up their minds whether we would bring bad or good luck to the village. This was no trivial matter to them and they were not taking any chances. Sometimes I would feel that I was being stared at. Faces would appear, and disappear quickly when I looked in their direction.

Every day the children of the village would run past the house. But their curiosity was always restrained by the warnings their parents gave about strangers. They never failed, as they ran by, to shout insults and curses. For them these were spells to ward off the evil eye, but I began to wonder if indeed there was not something evil in our presence in this calm landscape.

One afternoon a man came to see us. He had a little girl with him. He was our first civilian visitor. Once he had worked in my grandfather's stables and somehow he was not bound by the fears of the other villagers. He came, he said, to pay his respects to my mother and my aunt. While they talked, his daughter and I stared at each other. We were told to go outside and play, but both of us preferred to stay with the familiar.

This was the closest I had ever come to another child. I stared at her with such intensity that she became uneasy and hid in her father's arms. Throughout the entire visit we never said a word to each other. When it was time for them to leave the man leaned over my aunt and kissed her hand. He repeated this gesture with my mother. Then he turned to his daughter and asked her to do the same. I watched with fascination as she obeyed.

During these farewells I noticed that my mother and my aunt suddenly looked different. The presence of this man, a brief reminder of the past, had greatly affected them. A forgotten sense of pride seemed to have straightened their bodies and rearranged their shabby clothes.

Instinctively I adopted their pose. I felt my body stretching and becoming taller. I turned to the little girl and held out my hand. For a moment she hesitated, and then she imitated her father. The grown-ups smiled at us. From that moment on I felt more comfortable about my presence in the village. Now when the children rushed by our yard I stared at them openly. Their insults no longer meant anything to me.

Other thoughts held my interest. I found myself preoccupied by what seemed to me endless views of continuous space. Where did they begin or end, I wondered. What lay beyond these fields, these woods, at the point where details blurred on the horizon?

The village of Ochorna stood on a hilltop. Below it stretched the farmers' fields, subdivided by tall poplars. The wooden houses, leaning close together, formed a humble circle around the village church. I had never been near the church, but I could see its spire from our yard. It was the tallest structure in the village. I often tried to imagine how the land would look from such a height. In the distance I saw the bell tower of the next village. I visualized long rows of tall spires marching away from me to some unknown point. At other times I saw them as masts of ships, while the hills on which they stood became rolling waves, without beginning or end.

The more I thought about it the surer I became that this house, this yard, the animals, I and the people around me, were all at the very centre of the world. I promised myself that one day I would explore all the directions that radiated from me.

In this way the days passed, outwardly monotonous and alike. But inside myself I treasured the greatest of secrets. I had discovered a world beyond fear. I had also discovered my own being, just as another child might in his own house come upon a magnificent new toy whose existence he had never suspected.

V

TWO MONTHS LATER, the Russians were ready to advance. We were told to prepare to leave the village.

An army doctor came to see us towards the end of our stay. We were all examined. The news of my recovery was very good. The coughing had stopped, the lesions in my lungs were healing, and bones that had been twisted were growing straight. Everyone watched as the doctor made his diagnosis.

The old woman Marisia was there too. She crossed herself when the doctor spoke, and repeated "Thank God for this miracle" as a form of punctuation to his sentences.

He laughed at her. "No, old woman, your God had nothing to do with this. We all did it together. One day she will make us proud." He put an arm around me. "This child will grow up to do great things. Remember, I said so."

Every face smiled at me. I felt very fortunate. It

seemed to me then that there *was* something special about my life. I readily accepted the doctor's prophecy. With time it became a family theme. It was only when I grew up that I felt the full weight of the burden I had accepted so easily.

The Russian soldiers who came to see us were delighted with the change they saw. I had become their pet. They vied with each other in bringing me treats, in playing with me, and in making me laugh. They were all as proud of me as parents, but I had my favourite among them, Yuri, who had protected me the first day in the barn. When the time came to leave the village, I had no regrets. Yuri was going with us.

We set out early one morning. This time we were travelling with the soldiers in an army truck. The other survivors had left earlier with a convoy going in another direction. We were the only ones who wanted to return to Dobryd.

At last I was part of the noise and the laughter I had listened to with such wonder two months ago. So much had happened since then. We were about to resume the journey that began the day we left our loft. Yet now everything seemed different. In my mind the two were separated by a lifetime of change.

Djunek, Marisia and Kazia accompanied me to the truck. The old man gave us a bag of food for the trip, and the women cried. When the time came to say good-bye, their sobs and shouts of grief became more intense. *"Pani, pani,"* they cried as they clutched at my mother and my aunt. "Tell the Russians how we helped you. Don't forget us in the city."

My mother and my aunt, for all their suspicions, could not resist the mood of that morning. Even earlier in fact, towards the end of our stay, I had sensed a change in their attitude. These were after all the first people, after the soldiers, to treat us like human beings. Now they embraced us with feeling and promised to write. If any more proof were needed, this confirmed to all of us that fate had at last tipped its balance in our favour.

On the road, the village and farmhouse were quickly forgotten. The soldiers were eager to return to the front after their long rest. During this trip they were elated and full of confidence. While they joked and laughed together, my mother and my aunt sat tense and silent. I knew little of the fears and memories that preoccupied them as we travelled towards Dobryd. But I felt their tension and anxiety, and it affected me. Hope and dread mingled in my heart as I thought of our destination.

Yuri sat beside us. Like us, he felt the significance of this journey. To help the time pass he began to tell stories of the battles he had fought. Each one of the medals that he wore with such pride on his ragged uniform represented an incident of great courage. All his stories were simple, heroic tales of Russian daring. He told of the cowardice of the Germans who always became powerless in the end, faced with the courage of the Soviets. He told of the bravery and sacrifice of the Russian people, of their unsurpassable strength when their actions were directed by a common goal.

Throughout his narrative there was a message of confidence: we had all suffered and struggled but now the bad times were over. Now it was our turn to live in freedom and be happy. I had learned enough Russian in the last two months to understand the promise of Yuri's story. I believed it with all my heart. Much of it had already been fulfilled during the first weeks of freedom. Now that I was strong, I wanted to be as brave as Yuri and his comrades.

Two of his companions were women. It was the voice of one of them I had heard singing a familiar song the day we were liberated. Since then I had played with them many times. They were both young and cheerful, and very fond of playing tricks on the others. They seemed more like school girls than soldiers. Yet in battle, Yuri had assured us, they were often among the bravest in their unit. I looked at these girls as I listened to Yuri's stories and I promised myself that I would grow up like them—strong and unafraid. Ready to fight for a world where people lived free and happy.

A few hours later we entered the town. I knew immediately that something was not right. What I saw did not fit in with the glorious schemes Yuri had just drawn for our future.

In the morning we had left a village untouched by war. Now, a few hours later, we were driving through a town that was almost levelled. The village and the town seemed worlds apart.

Everywhere we looked we saw only ruins. Not one building appeared to be intact. Fires smouldered. Smoke hung in the air. We seemed to have arrived just at the end of some final battle.

The soldiers were as affected as the rest of us. For the first time I saw fear in their faces. Their rifles were raised and their eyes scanned the bombed-out buildings and the remaining rooftops. We met no resistance. In fact, it seemed we were the only ones alive in the town. People had either fled or remained trapped beneath the ruins which became their tombs. It was hard to imagine there had ever been any life here.

My mother and my aunt watched this spectacle as silently as the others. Occasionally, a hand would tremble or a shudder go through them when we passed the ruins of some familiar landmark. There was no longer any thought of finding their family home.

Their long ordeal was over but a new one was about to begin. Their hope of returning home died at the sight of the ruins. They were now truly homeless, condemned to live out the rest of their lives in a state of exile.

VI

"YOU CAN'T STAY in the town without our protection," Yuri was trying to explain to my mother. "There's nowhere you can go right now. You must come with us to the army camp. In a few days we'll clear away some of this mess and we'll find you a place to stay. Believe me, it looks worse than it is. I know. We've come into towns like this before, and in no time the place is rebuilt and bustling with life. You'll see, it will be the same here."

Yuri's face revealed the pain he felt as he spoke. It did not fit his words of optimism. It seemed almost comical to me to see him downcast like this. Was it a game, I wondered. Would he break into his usual smile in a minute and tease me about being fooled? I looked at his friends but their faces were also grim and closed. I withdrew further into our corner.

Now and then I heard Yuri curse to himself, softly, and his expression changed then from pain to anger. Again he turned to my mother and my aunt. It wasn't the destruction itself which upset him, he explained. He had seen little else in the last months of war. What angered him was that he and his comrades could not spare us this last blow.

"We'll build another Dobryd here. Finer than anything the Germans destroyed. We'll start from scratch. Everything will be new, modern. You'll see—we know how to build in Russia. We'll build a new town for a new kind of life. Yes, today is a sad day for you. But in six months, I promise you, we'll all be working so hard rebuilding this town that no one will have time to grieve."

If my mother and my aunt heard him, they gave no sign. They remained impassive, like the ruins about us. They were beyond words, beyond sympathy, cut off from other people's feelings by the darkness of their own.

We reached the army camp in the late afternoon. Yuri helped us out of the truck and we followed him inside. There we saw a large room with cots and blankets covering the floor space. The room was filled with people, other civilians, refugees like us who had nowhere to go.

People squeezed themselves together and somehow a corner was made for us. We were given straw mattresses. Someone brought us food and blankets. All the attention of the room was focused on us. After a few minutes some people came over to greet my mother and my aunt, but they received no response. They soon withdrew and after a while everyone left us alone.

In the days that followed the soldiers did their best to make us feel comfortable and welcome. They shared what they had and tried very hard to cheer everyone up. In the evening, one of them was always ready with a harmonica or a story. We were given daily bulletins on the progress of the war, and the victories of the Soviets were told in every detail.

My mother and my aunt took no part in this. They ate when food was brought, and they no longer cried, but they spoke to no one. Even the soldiers, all except Yuri, left them alone. Something about their withdrawal into grief made all attempts at consolation seem grotesque.

The grim foreboding of their entry into Dobryd was confirmed in the next few days. Most of their family was dead—parents, sisters, a brother, nieces, nephews and my father. Several people in the camp had witnessed his death.

At that time the news of his death meant nothing to me. We had been separated when I was just over two years old. I couldn't remember him at all. My mother had tried very hard to keep him alive for me, but I became uneasy whenever she spoke of him. I think it was because she herself could not speak of him without becoming very upset. My father had been her first love, the only one who had mattered. After the war there were other men, even one whom she married, yet throughout her life she continued to mourn for him, to talk of him, especially to me, his only child.

There were many stories, I remember, to illustrate his intelligence, his kindness, his love for her and for me. By the time I was an adolescent I had heard them all endless times. Her words became part of a family ritual, and I responded to them automatically, not listening, and without feeling. It was only when I grew up and left home that I thought of him as a real person. Someone who had actually lived. A man who had loved his wife, his child, his work. A man who had suffered, and died so young, at the age of thirty.

Nothing of him survived. For a long time there wasn't even a photograph to show me what he had looked like. We never found out what had happened to his body, so there was no grave to visit, just a vague memory I wasn't even sure was my own. Perhaps it came from one of my mother's stories. A man's face close to mine. A certain game we played. Bits and fragments, meaningless without the background that had been destroyed forever.

As an adult I finally did get to see a picture of him. I was visiting a distant cousin of his who lived in New York. We talked of my family, and I told her that I had often wondered about my father and regretted that no photographs of him had survived. She looked at me, surprised. "But I have some. I suppose I should have sent them to you long ago. But you know I never realized until this moment that you had no souvenir of him."

She returned with an old album. In the first photograph we found of my father he was shown with some university friends. They were on bicycles, with knapsacks on their backs, heading down a country road. In the next photograph he was playing chess with a friend, his face in profile as he concentrated on the game. There was one more picture, larger than the other two, and obviously more professional. He and my mother, on their wedding trip, posed for the camera in St. Mark's Square in Venice while pigeons settled around them. My mother and my father looked incredibly young, happy, her arm through his, their hands clasped.

I asked my cousin if I could keep the photographs. Later that night, back in my hotel room, I spread them out before me and stared at them for a long time. I tried to connect these images with those already embedded in my mind. But it was no good. Too many of the connecting links were gone, destroyed forever. Then I cried, from fatigue and frustration. I cried for the young man in these pictures, and also for myself because I had never known him. I suppose that night, so many years after that day in camp when I had learned of his death, I finally mourned for my father.

The only happy event during those first weeks in Dobryd was the return of my father's brother, still in his Russian army uniform. But when we were reunited I did not think of it as a joyful occasion. Somehow in my mind my uncle's return became associated with the state of grief that my aunt and my mother suffered. What was coincidental became for me cause and effect. For a long time I resented his presence.

The weeks in the army camp were very unhappy for me, even worse than the time in the loft. What frightened me most was that my family had forgotten about me. For weeks on end they sat silently together, so lost in their grief that they took no notice of me. Eventually, however, they became aware of me again. One day I noticed that they were responding to me as they used to, treating me with the attentiveness that I had assumed was my right. Slowly they began to notice the activity around them.

Life in the camp had taken on an intense pitch. The town was being restored. People were rebuilding their lives. My family realized they had to rouse themselves.

Yet there remained some distance between them and the other refugees. Several times I overheard people in the camp telling stories about them. Those who knew the family before the war spoke of my grandfather. Of how he had lived as the largest land-owner in the area. They told the others that the family were never like other Jews. There was always something foreign and aloof about them. They were too assimilated, too rich, and they travelled too much.

I noticed that when these stories were told, certain people did not hesitate to express satisfaction that the war had reduced everyone to the same level. I began to feel very uncomfortable in the camp. I longed for us to leave, to be on our own. My mother agreed. Yuri promised to help us.

During the short time in the camp I had lost some of my confidence in the new world of freedom. People were neither happy nor good to each other as Yuri had promised. Would they ever be?

PART TWO

I

I WAS GLAD to leave the army camp. Yet the move
back to Dobryd filled me with uneasiness. My first
impressions of our entry into the town were still vivid:
the death-like stillness, the ruins, the absence of other
people. I had never seen anything so desolate. How
would we survive in a place where all human activity
seemed unimaginable?

I said nothing of this to my mother or my aunt.
I sensed that I must not add to their feelings of hope-
lessness.

My fears disappeared as soon as we returned to
the town. In our absence, Dobryd had been transformed into a city for the living. Bombed-out buildings, piles of rubble, caverns gouged out by hands—all
had become shelters. Everywhere we went, people
swarmed over the ruins, determined to survive.

They began to arrive almost as soon as the Germans
had retreated. At first singly, furtively, then *en masse*,
as if a common signal of confidence had spread
amongst them. Ragged, emaciated, with small precious bundles of unlikely objects, they came into the
town in steady streams of life that defied the ruins.
Every corner of the town pulsed with activity. A new

community was created. Even those who remembered the elaborate pre-war civilization that had flourished here seemed too preoccupied with reconstruction to mourn it. In this new Dobryd, my optimism about the future returned once again.

At last we had a home of our own. In the midst of a street of ruins Yuri had discovered an intact wing of an apartment house. People were already living there when we arrived, but we managed to find a space that would be ours alone.

The rooms we claimed were filled with rubble, and it took us several days to clean them out. I loved the work, sifting the dirt, filling up buckets of it, and carrying it outside. When we were finished I was very proud of our effort. It seemed to me that we had made a splendid home for ourselves. There was no glass in the windows, nor did we have water or electricity, but the rooms were large and comfortable. I was particularly excited by some of the objects we had discovered hidden in the rubble. To me these simple artifacts of domestic life seemed like treasures.

The find most prized by everyone was a wood stove. On the rare occasions when there was firewood to burn we would gather near it with our neighbours and Yuri's friends. We sat closely around it, and as the stove heated up it became very warm in the room. Faces grew flushed and perspiration dotted foreheads, yet no one moved away. The heat could not be too intense. Everyone in the room believed in its curative powers. Our guests seemed to become more expansive with the rising temperature, responding to it as if it were a stimulant. Occasionally someone would bring a few sugar cubes and then the evening became a true party.

I was still the only child amongst adults. Extra pieces

of sugar were saved for me, but otherwise I was ignored. This meant I could stay and listen to the grown-ups as long as I wished, until I fell asleep in their midst. If anyone tried to move me from the floor onto the straw mattress where I slept, I always protested. I wanted to remain as long as I could within the circle of warmth, lulled by the conversation of the adults around me.

These evenings, however, did not occur very often. Our family and everyone we knew devoted all energy to the hunt for food. The city itself had been sucked dry of its resources. The Red Army distributed rations to keep the population from starving. These were so inadequate that hunger remained a constant complaint. The army itself was no better off than the civilians it fed; there simply was not enough to go around. What complicated matters even more was the way in which the army distributed its rations. Somehow this process occurred in a senseless and confusing fashion, so that, for example, while some people received only flour, others would receive nothing but packages of yeast. As a result, everyone was forced to spend most of their time in long and tedious sessions of barter and exchange.

Hunger was frequently accompanied by the prevailing disease of the time: dysentery. We all endured it with resignation. It was as much a part of the climate of our lives as the war-blemished landscape in which we lived.

This common affliction created a new pastime. People perfected their own private remedies and discussed them endlessly with their neighbours. There was no proper medication, and people turned to home remedies, peasant cures and the inventions of their imagination.

In our house the favourite treatment consisted of charcoal. Twice a week, my mother would carefully heat some precious pieces of wood. When these were partly burned and charred, she ground them into a black bitter powder. I can still recall its taste, harsh, lingering, unlike anything else. I also remember with what violence I resisted the mandatory daily dose. Everything about it revolted me, but there was no escaping it. Tears, screams, gagging brought no reprieve. My protests were ignored. Both my mother and my aunt, normally so indulgent with me, were not to be moved in this instance. Sooner or later they would have their way and I would be forced to swallow that dreadful substance. The nauseous after-taste remained for hours, to remind me that the ordeal would have to be repeated the following day.

I think that I was as hurt by my aunt's and my mother's severity as I was revolted by the horrid taste of black powder on my tongue. I could not understand why they were not moved by my pleas. Years later I realized that their unyielding insistence on this particular ritual was for them a desperate act of self-assurance. Since they had nothing else to give me, it was important for them to believe it worked.

Sometimes, strange, out-of-place events occurred, or so they seemed to me at the time. Echoes of an unknown world which excited my imagination. Once, in the course of an ordinary day, word spread through our building that ice-cream was being sold. Soon hordes of children came rushing past our window shouting with excitement. Immediately, I wanted to join them, without really understanding what the excitement was all about.

"Wait." My mother grabbed at me. "There's no use going unless you have something to exchange." I waited impatiently as she searched through our few belongings.

Just then Yuri walked in. He had brought us a precious tin of meat as a gift. After a brief conversation, the adults agreed to sacrifice this gift for my first taste of ice-cream. I knew enough about our life to realize that such an exchange was not made lightly. Without explanation I understood the importance of this event and I was deeply impressed.

It was not safe for me to walk through the town alone with my prize and so Yuri decided to go with me. He held my hand as we followed the noise of the children who were somewhere ahead of us, out of sight. I scarcely noticed the landscape of ruins we passed. It was simply the place where I lived, to be taken for granted.

We were approaching the centre of the noise. We pushed our way through the crowd to a doorway. Just inside it an old man and a young woman sat beside a wooden barrel wrapped in rags and paper. Yuri handed over our tin of meat while I held out the saucepan I had taken from home. The woman took it from me, bent over the barrel, and filled my pan with a creamy white substance.

Yuri led me away from the crowd and into a deserted doorway. We sat down inside it. I tasted my precious purchase and I was not disappointed. It lived up to my expectations. Yuri urged me to eat it faster, before it all melted, but nothing on earth would have induced me to rush through this experience. I lingered over each mouthful, rested between them, and Yuri, resigned, leaned back and watched me. Every time I looked up he smiled back at me. "Don't worry," he said, "soon there will be ice-cream every day for all children." I had utter faith in Yuri, but just this once I doubted him. I could not believe that what I was experiencing at the moment could become part of the everyday world as I knew it.

In the evening, Yuri described our adventure to my mother. When he came to the part where I first tasted the ice-cream, I laughed with them as Yuri's face mimicked my own. But my interest shifted quickly from his expression to my mother's. My mother was laughing and I suddenly realized that I had never heard her laugh this way before. She looked different. Younger, prettier. I would have done anything to keep her as she was at that moment. I tried to clown, exaggerating Yuri's mimicry, turning to any comic gesture that I could invent, but already her face had changed into the familiar set expression that I saw every day. The moment had passed.

Yuri and my mother were talking of something else, and no one paid any further attention to me for the rest of the evening. But I was not discouraged. The taste of ice-cream and the brief glimpse of my mother behind her mask of worry and grief were such important events to me that I felt myself protected by them from our desperate day-to-day reality.

Another event, equally strange and wonderful.

My mother, my aunt, Yuri and I are inside a large tent, filled with people. We are surrounded by soldiers but there are a few women as well in civilian dress. They seem to be particularly shabby in the midst of the crispness and shine of the army uniforms. At first I don't see any children, but then Yuri lifts me onto his knees and I notice a few.

I don't know what to expect but I feel very excited. It seems to me that everyone around me shares my mood. The lights dim, we are sitting in darkness, but below us the wooden platform is strongly illuminated. Something is going to happen there, I realize, and I keep my eyes fixed on the spot of light so as not to miss anything.

At last a man appears in the light. He welcomes us to the army show and tells of the marvellous entertainment that will follow. I become so excited that I can hardly sit still. There will be singers and dancers, he tells us, who have come all the way from Moscow just to entertain us. Some soldiers from the camp will also perform a special act created for this evening. The clapping and cheering become very loud. Then at a sign from the man, everyone becomes silent. The show begins.

There are no sets, no props, no costumes. The performers, like most of the audience, are dressed in uniforms. Yet I know immediately that what is happening on the platform has no relation to anything I have ever seen. Such is the power of the mood created by the performers that I feel myself carried away from my everyday self. I forget that it ever existed. I'm part of the beauty and magic that is being created before me. It seems to me that the people who are on the stage making this happen must be the happiest people in the world.

Suddenly I realize that everyone around me is laughing. The singers and dancers have left the stage. In their place there is a man dressed in a suit much too large for him. His shoes are so long he keeps tripping over them. His clothes seem borrowed from a fat giant. He is joined by two women wearing dresses that touch the floor, so long that their feet become entangled in the folds. The three of them seem to be imitating the dancers who preceded them, but they only succeed in tripping each other and stumbling into each other's arms.

I ask my mother why everyone is laughing. "It is because of the clothes," my mother answers. I have never seen such clothes. "They came from America," my mother tells me, "in CARE packages." But they are either so inappropriate or so outsized that they have become a popular symbol of post-war humour.

I still don't understand what is causing the laughter I hear, but everyone around me recognizes the skit. It seems to me that the audience is laughing at the actors and I find this laughter cruel. The people in the circle of light are part of the evening's magic—sacred creatures to be revered and not laughed at.

It soon becomes obvious to me that the actors themselves are contributing to this sacrilege. They have become awkward creatures trapped in their hazardous clothes. They stumble, trip, and fall over one another. The costumes are trampled, ripped and soon in shreds. At the end, the actors are dressed only in ludicrous rags. I feel sad. It all seems such a terrible waste. Why didn't anyone stop them, I wonder.

The show is over and I'm very sleepy. On the way home I fall asleep. But when I'm put to bed I wake up again. I remember what troubled me. I cannot let my mother leave the room unless she explains it to me. Most important, I must find out if the clothes have been ruined forever.

"Silly girl." My mother laughs. "What a thing to worry about."

But I do. In the world of scarcity that I know, the destruction I have just witnessed seems to me tragic. Surely the actors must feel as sad as I do now. My

mother laughs at my sorrow, but when she sees that
I will not sleep she tries to reassure me.

"Come now, there's no need for you to be sad. They
were only pretending to tear their clothes. The way
you pretend in your games. The actors tear at loose
seams without really harming the clothes. Now you
can stop worrying and go to sleep."

My mother leaves. I'm no longer worried but I still
can't sleep. I relive the entire show in my head. Without knowing it, I'm creating a ceremony that will stay
with me for many years. From that night on, as soon
as I'm in bed, I call forth dancers, singers, comics,
and they perform for me alone. I fall asleep at night
to the sound of applause and laughter.

II

THE CENTRE OF my life in Dobryd was the marketplace.

Ochorna, the village where we had lived
immediately after our release, had seemed to me then
enormously complex and exciting. Now I saw it as
small and restricted in comparison to the experiences
Dobryd offered. Within Dobryd, the marketplace
superimposed itself on everything that had come
before and blotted it out.

In the morning, as soon as I opened my eyes, I
would remember that in a little while my aunt and
I would go there and I would be filled with a pleasant
sense of anticipation. Outside, the streets were already
alive with people coming into town to trade. I was
impatient to join them and I would rush my aunt

through her morning chores so that we could leave as early as possible.

Ours, I later realized, was characteristic of many other markets that flourished immediately after the war. The people who gathered there came to carry on the ordinary desperate business of life that was typical of those times. To me, however, there was nothing ordinary or sad about what happened here. Each day, as I sat beside my aunt in the little kiosk where she sold some of the extra supplies my mother and Yuri procured for her, what I saw seemed to me exciting, new and completely engrossing.

All this activity took place on a vast square of ground that still contained the outline of the buildings that had once stood there. As soon as it was cleared of the ruins, the first stalls appeared. These were erected practically overnight, with great ingenuity, from the materials that lay scattered about. Soon the entire square was covered with shops. When all the vacant space was used up the original builders began to lease parts of their kiosks to those who arrived after them.

The peasants, who had at first stayed away from the town, began to explore the possibilities of trading in the marketplace. Early in the summer they began to come into town with their supplies, which they had kept well-hidden. For the first time since our arrival we saw fresh butter, eggs and vegetables for sale. These were greeted with the kind of excitement that must have welcomed the first merchant traders back from China.

The square was filled with noise and activity from dawn till dark. Everyone came: civilians, refugees, peasants, soldiers, nuns from a nearby convent, transients making their way west towards Germany or east to Russia, the old, the young, and even the few stray dogs that had survived to return here stubbornly in spite of the harsh reception that met them daily.

People came for food, clothes, furnishings, entertainment. They came for papers and passports. They bought new identities and acquired convenient new families. They came looking for work, for travel permits, for anything at all. Many of them came and stayed without purpose—a silent crowd of onlookers whose arrivals and departures went without notice. Whatever the need, the market was everyone's best hope.

Scraps of information were valued as highly as goods, and people paid dearly to learn facts concerning their friends and relatives. It often turned out that they had been tricked or lied to, but this did not prevent others from taking their place and paying for similar information.

Sometimes it did happen that people who had given up hope of seeing each other again were reunited among the stalls. Such meetings were of course very rare. Yet everyone who came to the marketplace lived in anticipation of them. Emotions always ran high, and every new arrival quickened the hopes of the many who lived in uncertainty.

When my aunt and I first came to the marketplace the only goods we saw came either from the Soviet army's supply stores or from scavengers who spent their time sifting through the ruins. Then the peasants began to arrive and everything changed. They brought with them not only their farm produce but also a rich variety of luxury items, hidden or left in their safekeeping by some of Dobryd's wealthiest citizens.

Most of these objects were strange to me. I had

no idea what function they had once performed. I approached them as displays in a museum, all the more mysterious since they lay there without any form of identification. I wandered among them, fascinated and intrigued. I vaguely sensed that I had come upon the remains of a civilization which, although quite foreign to me now, had once been a part of my life.

In the weeks following the German retreat, the peasants realized that there was little chance that rightful owners would return to retrieve possessions stored in haste before fleeing. The few who had survived and did manage to return usually lacked the strength to assert their claim to any of their former possessions. The peasants became more and more daring. Precious, luxurious objects filled their stalls. Very quickly we all became accustomed to seeing these items displayed side by side with the more familiar vegetables and sacks of grain.

When my aunt had sold the few things she brought with her in the morning, she would take my hand and we would wander in the alleys of the marketplace, this time as potential buyers or spectators.

On our way we would pass stacks of fine linen, handmade lace tablecloths and samplers of intricate embroidery. All this, my aunt would explain as she identified the objects for me, might have belonged to a bride's trousseau, started in childhood. Elsewhere, we would come upon displays of silverware with the monograms or seals of their former owners blatantly exposed. Stocky peasant women, their hair tied up in flowered scarves, sat in the midst of shops filled with the loot of war. Casually, as they chatted with each other, their hands would stray to the nearby objects, settling for a moment on some delicate silver or gold combs, picking up some small box, inlaid and encrusted with jewels, passing with indifference over the beautifully carved hair brushes, the matching hand mirrors, the gold chains weighted by pocket watches that no one bothered to wind.

I could have remained before these objects for hours if my aunt hadn't prodded me on. She, who had grown up in luxury and comfort, walked impassively past these riches, or so it seemed to me.

"Look over there!" I would shout, pulling at her hand to direct her attention at something that had caught my eye. "Yes, yes, I see," she would answer in a tone of voice that told me that she could not possibly have seen what I meant. I would become more insistent, demanding that her excitement match my own. Finally, growing impatient, she would take hold of my hand and firmly pull me in another direction.

I could not understand her lack of interest. Yet other shoppers ignored them as well. I noticed that many people looked away when they came close to these luxuries. For the most part they were the playthings of the farmers' children. I became certain that there was a mysterious story attached to these objects, some secret that the grown-ups did not want to talk about. It was hard not to pester my aunt with questions, even though I sensed that they made her uncomfortable. There was so much to see, however, that my attention never stayed fixed on one object for long.

When we had finished our purchases, we usually walked over to the section of the market where prepared foods were sold. Throughout the day, the odours of cooking that came from this area pervaded the entire market. Since everyone was usually hungry, the effect of these smells was highly intoxicating. The briskest trade, the quickest turnover, occurred here.

My aunt, who could never bear to disappoint me, would urge me to choose something, even though we both knew the extravagance would annoy my mother. The choice was not easy. There were so many things I liked. The dishes the farmers made were the kind they normally ate themselves—some combination of flour and potatoes flavoured with fried onions or cabbage. There was a dessert that I particularly liked—deep-fried slices of apple—called apples-in-pyjamas. The name was the chief reason I chose it so often.

The day passed quickly for me. When it grew dark we made our way home. Often my mother and Yuri would already be there waiting for us. If they were not too tired, or too preoccupied with other matters, I would be allowed to tell about my day in the market. I loved those moments. We sat around the table and I held their attention with my words. It would have been hard for me to decide at that time which I enjoyed more—the experience itself or the opportunity it gave me for reworking that experience into a story.

At this time the marketplace seemed to me all wonder and enchantment. I saw it with the eyes of a five-year-old. But somehow, while I created games and stories around it, my mind also absorbed other kinds of information which at the time I could not understand. Years later I realized that the transactions of the marketplace, the ordinary daily events that had filled my imagination, had had a deep, long-lasting influence. They were my first lessons in the rules of life and I did not forget them. Many of the discoveries I made later in life seemed to have been foreshadowed by the events I watched from my aunt's booth in the marketplace.

III

WE WERE SETTLED in Dobryd and our life had acquired its own rhythm. We had our home, my mother worked for the Russians as a translator, and my aunt spent her days in the marketplace, selling and trading. My uncle had returned to his regiment and it was some time before he rejoined us. I had no school to go to, and so for the most part I did as I pleased.

I was never lonely or bored. My days were filled with the excitement of constant discovery. For one thing, at about this time I became involved with other children for the first time in my life. At first there were no children in our building, but the street was full of them—children who roamed the town in gangs of all ages, ignored by everyone else.

Where had they come from, I wondered. Who were they? Somehow I had always known that other children existed, even during the days in the loft. But this was different. They were not as I had imagined them. Nothing in my past had prepared me for the experience of actually being with them, sharing their games, becoming a part of their world. I was something of a freak amongst them. I could read and write and recite long poems and keep still for hours, but I had no idea what children did when they played together, nor what it meant to be part of a group. I came to them with the conception of myself as a unique, solitary person, distinct and separate from all others. It never occurred to me that I might find my likeness in another being.

But these children seemed not to notice anything peculiar or special about me. I was just another kid, in a world where the word "normal" had lost its meaning. When I was with them, running down a street, I felt that for that moment we were all alike. My own private self seemed to fall away, and I felt myself change, blending physically with other arms and legs that mimicked my own, with voices that drowned mine.

Sometimes it seemed to me that I was two people—one running, laughing, indistinguishable from the rest, the other, hidden, watching, marvelling at their freedom and my own abandonment.

In the days that followed I acquired two particular friends of my own. A Russian boy, Kolek, and a Polish girl, Eva. They were about six years old, as I was by then, and lived nearby. They had always played with other children and they accepted our new friendship quite casually. I, however, found myself in a constant state of excitation when I was with them. I could not grasp how they understood each other so well, or how they knew what each expected of the other. Yet, very quickly, I was behaving with similar ease with them. I became familiar with the language of children, and passed from observer to participant.

It was understood between us that our friendship had to exist outside our homes and unknown to our families. We only sensed the hatred and the painful memories so prevalent in the minds of adults around us. We realized, however, that in our joy in each other we possessed something uncommon to the times, and we treasured it.

We seldom visited one another's homes. We knew very little about one another's lives outside of our play group. Our families left us alone, thankful that we managed to stay out of their hair. In our post-war world, the distinctions between conquerors, refugees and vanquished were blurred in the common struggle to keep one's body fed and covered and one's bed warm. Beyond that there was little energy left over. We children were mostly ignored and forgotten.

Our games were played in the ruins of the buildings around us, or in the streets, where the barricades of the city's last defence became our hideout. Holding each other's hands and helping each other over obstacles, we explored the nearby ruins. Almost all civilians lived by scavenging, and the ruins had already been well-picked for anything that could be used or sold. Yet we managed to find objects either overlooked or unwanted by previous scavengers. We treasured these and hid them in secret places. Occasionally we would bring out our finds with great caution and reverence, as we had seen the peasants bring out a treasured relic on feast days.

Amongst our prizes there were some photographs. The people in them were strangers and they posed in happy groups at long-past family celebrations. We were especially interested in the children in these pictures, the clothes they wore, the way their hair was combed, the toys they sometimes held. We invented names for them and thought of them as our friends.

One photograph in particular intrigued me. It showed a beautiful, elaborate merry-go-round, its arrested movement while children sat astride them, holding on to their harnesses or their necks. None ornamented horses caught in different positions of of us had ever been to an amusement park. Nor did we know what a merry-go-round was. But we needed no explanations. The expressions on the faces of the children in the photograph assured us we were looking at something which caused great pleasure. Through the photograph we somehow felt as if we were sharing this pleasure. We treasured it and took turns making up stories about what it portrayed.

The adults in the photographs intrigued us as well. They were the visual echoes of a past we would never know. So little of it had imprinted itself on us that we could look at these photographs without nostalgia, but with the curiosity of small savages confronted with mysterious artifacts.

In time we became quite possessive about the people in the photographs. They were no longer anonymous faces. We gave them names, and a sense of familiarity grew out of our longings. Each one of us lived in a household that represented the broken remnants of ordinary family life. The missing members were constantly evoked for us by the adults, and we lived with their faceless, ghost-like presences. In our photographs we found characters to people our, ghost-ridden homes. Soon we disputed among ourselves about these smiling images, each claiming them for his or her family tree.

A piece of flimsy white material found in the rubble of a nearby building became another of our special treasures. We did not know where it came from. Possibly it had once been a part of someone's white tulle curtains. It became to us our magic mantle. When any one of us carried it we felt ourselves invested with the presence of the people and the events we re-enacted through our games.

One of our favourite games originated in an event portrayed in the photographs. It was a wedding party on the point of leaving church after the ceremony. We knew little of what this meant but we understood that it was a celebration of some kind. Lacking precise details we recreated our own version of this event with immense pleasure. Our bit of tulle became a bridal veil. Around it we created a sequence of events which became increasingly elaborate and complex. After a time we began to have difficulty in remembering all the steps required in the rites we ourselves had invented.

Unlike ordinary children we did not parody reality. Somehow we had an enormous need to forget it. Instead of recreating the roles of adults as we saw them, we preferred fantasy and invention. Yet there was little to encourage us in that direction. We had to rely totally on our own resources, and these seemed to bloom in response to our needs. Our times together were filled with rich and inventive games that I recall, even now, with pleasure.

From that time on, fantasy-playing became an essential daily routine of my life. When my friends were not around I carried on by myself. I never thought of it as an escape or a substitute for the sad drabness of our life. For me it was part of the reality of our life, just as much as my visits to the marketplace or the stories my aunt told me about the past.

I grew up thinking that all children spent their free time in this way, participating vigorously in an imaginary world that was as vivid as anything that they actually experienced. It came as a great surprise to me in later years to discover how different other people's childhoods had been.

PART THREE

I

LIFE INSIDE OUR flat was beginning to change. Inevitably, like everyone around us, my family was making its adjustments to the world in which we lived. Their behaviour acquired a semblance of conformity, and I was relieved that we were no longer avoided as we had been in the army camp. For the time being, the past which separated my mother and aunt from other survivors had been successfully camouflaged.

I began to notice a change in them. While I had been totally occupied with exploring the world of children, games, the streets, the marketplace, they had returned to life. I suddenly realized that not only could I become like other children but they too were beginning to resemble, more and more each day, other "normal" adults.

Now when we walked together through the streets of Dobryd, they were indistinguishable from other passers-by. Like everyone else they wore drab army-surplus clothes. Their hair was long, braided and twisted around their heads in thick coronets. Their bodies were no longer skeletal, but filled out and rounded like my own. Their anonymity was further enhanced by the fact that the post-war population of Dobryd was almost entirely new. People did not talk easily about their former lives. Old social and class distinctions had no meaning in this setting. My mother and my aunt were treated by their neighbours with the familiarity of equals, and they in turn were content not to evoke the past in the presence of strangers.

When the three of us were alone, however, it was another matter. Then the present receded like a clever but flimsy backdrop. My mother and my aunt abandoned their ordinary, everyday masks worn for outsiders, and became different people. With my aunt as guide, I was led away from the familiar, in another direction: towards the past. Not the immediate past which I remembered vaguely, but to a time further back whose distance from the present seemed to me inconceivable.

Slowly, over a period of months, through different, often unrelated stories, I became aware of a remote world, the world that had vanished before my birth. I still continued to live in the present, and in the intervals between my aunt's stories I often forgot about the other world, but somehow I was no longer as satisfied with the present as I had been before the stories began.

Even at that early age, I resented that other world which returned to mock my own. When I grew older, it seemed to me that all my particular problems had their source in this profound gulf between the present and the past, across which I was expected to build a new life. At different times I turned against one and then the other, pretending in turn that they didn't matter, until I felt forced to admit that they did. In any case, in both worlds I always thought of myself as an intruder, an imposter, doomed to live in perpetual exile.

II

IT ALL BEGAN innocently enough with my aunt's attempts to amuse and distract me by telling stories whenever I was being difficult or impatient. In no time at all I was addicted, hanging on to her every word, begging her to go on and on.

The first stories are associated in my mind with an unpleasant routine, which makes their content particularly unreal and troubling for me.

The table has been cleared, the kerosene lamp removed from its hook on the wall and placed on the table. A familiar procedure is about to begin, one which I both look forward to and dislike: the light is used to search out the lice in my hair. To take my mind off this activity which I find so tedious, my aunt will amuse me with storytelling.

The only thing that keeps the lice partly under control are these nightly searches. My mother is by now very good at this work. Every time she spots a louse she lowers the lamp and I feel the slight crunch as it is squashed between her thumbnails.

Eventually I become impatient. I don't want to keep still. My head hurts from leaning back. But it's not time for me to get up. The acceptable quota of dead lice for each evening has not been reached. My aunt is called to help out.

She pulls her chair over so that she is sitting facing

me, but because of the way I'm sitting, I can't see her face. My eyes are on the ceiling but after a while I get tired of watching the insect colony that thrives up there. I prefer to close my eyes and "see" my aunt's story. Her voice, detached from her face, seems to come from far away. Her stories are never the kind that begin "once upon a time". They are "real," but the effect is the same.

Above all, my aunt preferred the stories of her youth. Perhaps like all children I once said to her "Please tell me about when you were a little girl," and a pattern between us was established.

We have returned to the beginning of this century. She is a young girl again, describing the joys of summer holidays spent in the family's country home:

"I was always sad when summer ended. It seems to me I lived from one summer to the next, wishing the time in between would pass more quickly. Not that I didn't like school in Vienna. The teachers were very nice to me. I had many friends. On Sundays I went to your grandfather's cousin's house, where there were always a lot of young people and parties and dances. Vienna itself was a beautiful, rich city. There was so much to see and do. The one afternoon a week we were allowed to go out on our own seemed all too short.

"None of this compared, however, to the way I felt about our country house. You see, I was born in it, and I could still remember what it was like living there all year around. Your mother was only a baby when your grandfather moved into town for the winters. I was the oldest and I could remember what it had been like. To live in any other place seemed like a cruel banishment to me, and afterwards, whenever

I saw the house again, at the beginning of each summer, I felt my exile more deeply than ever. But there was also joy, the joy of coming home after a long absence.

"When we arrived, the servants who lived in the house were already outside waiting for us. As soon as our carriage stopped, a little girl, no bigger than you are now, would come forward to welcome us with bread and salt. I was always the first out and such was my excitement that I had to kiss everyone near me. They would kiss me back with equal enthusiasm.

"In our house there was none of the awkwardness that usually separates servants and masters. It was such a happy household. Some of the younger women had been my playmates when we were children and they felt quite free to tease me about how much I'd grown, what a young lady I'd become, and how my father had better find me a husband before I was an old maid. They, of course, were all married by then, and some had children. These things happened very early in the village. This difference in experience separated us as much as any class differences—perhaps more so. As married women they belonged to a secret world, and until I was initiated into it there were all sorts of things they couldn't talk about before me. Nevertheless, I still felt as close to them as I used to when we all played together.

"The only person who disapproved of this was your grandmother. As a matter of fact, she objected to a lot of things that were part of our life in the country. She never really felt comfortable away from the city or her relatives. We were the only Jewish landowners in the area and she feared her children were becoming assimilated. Every spring when it was time to prepare for the move she would complain and look for excuses not to go. Your grandfather, I think, was quite capable of leaving her behind for the summer and in the end this always forced her to come along. Once we were there, however, even she softened a bit.

"The house itself was just an ordinary large manor house joined to the village below it by a long avenue of old lime trees. It was its setting and the life we had there that made it so special for me. It stood in the midst of flower gardens, berry bushes, and rows upon rows of fruit trees. The odour that came from these as they flowered was one of the great attractions of living in the house. The beehives behind the orchard produced a honey that tasted like no other I've ever had. I suppose it had something to do with the richness and variety of the blossoms. Beyond these were the woods, where as children we used to play and hide, and where we learned all about picking mushrooms.

"Once a year your great-great aunt from Cracow arrived at our country house to gather certain leaves and herbs that grew in the nearby forest. I remember she never allowed us to go with her on these expeditions. We would try to follow but she always spotted us and made us go back. I don't know what she picked; it was all very mysterious. So were the preparations she made from her pickings. No one ever learned what exactly went into each one. None of us, I suppose, was considered sufficiently gifted to be entrusted with her secret formulas.

"The family treated her as something of a joke. Especially the so-called enlightened members, who despised all local customs and traditions. To them she was a source of embarrassment. Still, she had a great reputation. People came from all over to seek her help and buy her preparations. They certainly worked for her. She remained vigorous and attractive as long as I knew her. Who knows how much longer she could have lived? I remember how she danced with all the young men at your mother's wedding.

"The last time I saw her was the day after you were born. She arrived at your grandfather's house and placed a special necklace around your neck. Baltic amber I think it was, but it wasn't an ordinary necklace of course. Then she was off, without stopping even for a glass of tea. Too many people needed her she said. She was ninety-three when the Germans shot her.

"The necklace? Manya, our seamstress, got it. It wasn't very valuable but she wanted it because it came from your great-great aunt. Peasants like Manya were in great awe of her.

"Where was I? Yes, the house. After a quick run through the garden I would turn to the house. Each room received a short inspection, and the best, my own room, was saved for the last. Then I was in it, and it was just as it had always been, except that the shutters were closed, waiting for me to open them. Beyond lay the richness of the fields, the rooftops of the village, and the mountains. Now I had really come home.

"The days passed quickly, much quicker than in town or at school. What did we do? Let me think. Oh, so many things.

"Well, for one thing, there was all the work that was part of the summer and harvesting. I didn't really have to help but I wanted to. We picked mushrooms, strung them in garlands and hung them up to dry in attic rooms. We gathered baskets full of wild roses for syrups and jams. They seemed to grow more abundantly each year. Then there were berries to pick—red and white currants, gooseberries and blueberries. Some were used for preserves; others were set aside to ferment and eventually were made into liqueurs. The farmers brought us their choicest vegetables, and these too were preserved in glass jars for the winter.

"We were a large family, but over the year we scarcely dented the supplies that were stored at the end of summer in the cellars and pantries. Yet each summer there was the same frantic activity to lay aside more and more preserves. I suppose most of it was habit, but there was also a great generosity in those times. There was always a steady stream of beggars, wanderers and gypsies at our back door who were fed and equipped with supplies. No one was ever turned away empty-handed, and we never went visiting without taking along a basket full of samples from our garden.

"The same useless abundance applied to our linen and undergarments. At some point during our stay, the village seamstress would arrive and move into the house. She would sew all day long, making linens, shifts, towels. There was already enough linen in that house to last us a lifetime. Still, every summer, a new supply was made to fill yet another closet.

"The room where the seamstress worked was usually filled with women, friends of hers who dropped in to keep her company, and some of the servants who wanted to learn from her. There was always a pot of tea brewing, and everyone kept busy working and talking. Whatever the seamstress finished we embroidered with the family's initials, and everything had to be trimmed with the hand-made lace that we all worked on constantly. Downstairs, the servants worked hard plucking geese, preparing the down, and packing it into the huge linen quilts and pillowcases that we sewed upstairs.

"As you see, there really was a lot to do. And since I didn't have to do any of it, the fun for me lay in starting one thing, dropping it for another, picking it up again when the hard part had been done by someone else and getting all sorts of compliments for my skills. When I got tired of that there was time for reading, long walks, picnics and visiting. The possibilities of my life seemed endless there, except that it all went so fast—much too fast for me.

"Then, when the fields were most beautiful, thick, golden and swaying, it was time for me to set out for school.

"My trunk was packed with new clothes, delicacies from our kitchen, presents for my teachers and our cousins, but I participated in none of this. It was too painful for me to prepare my own banishment. I really couldn't see it any other way. Especially since I was the first to leave. The others stayed on for another two weeks, when the young children returned to Dobryd. How I envied them. In fact, when it was time for me to leave I would have gladly changed places with anyone in the village.

"At last the day of my departure would arrive. I would wake up to the mournful looks of the servants. For them, all separations were fatal. Our finest horses, all the same height and size, of a uniform grey colour, would be brought out and harnessed. Your grandfather, knowing how sad I felt, would drive me to the train himself. I was indifferent to it all. I watched the house disappear from view. I looked at the fields which we drove through, the farmers who bowed to

us as we passed, and already I missed them as if I
were a long way from home.

"On the train I would eat the food that had been
packed for me, feeling very sorry for myself, thinking
of the others still in the house, probably having a
great time, my presence among them already forgotten. During those first painful hours of separation
I consoled myself with the promises I made about
the future. Once I was grown up, nothing would keep
me from living there whenever I wanted to. It was
inconceivable to me then that anything could happen
that would prevent me from keeping the promise I
made to myself.

"How foolish such faith in the future seems now.
But at that time I wasn't the only one to feel that
way. We all did. We thought that life would always
go on as we knew it. Who could have foreseen what
lay ahead of us? Such horrors were without' precedent."

My mother had given up searching my scalp. We were
both listening to my aunt. My mother, growing into
adolescence fifteen years later than my aunt, had had
an entirely different youth. She had always been
drawn to the socialist and revolutionary ideas of her
time. As a result she had a more critical impression
of her bourgeois childhood. As a young girl her
activities had been very different from those that kept
my aunt in the company of other women, delighting
in the traditional tasks of a young lady. Yet the spell
of my aunt's nostalgia was so powerful that she never
interrupted. In any case, now that it was all gone,
destroyed, there was no point in correcting my aunt's
reminiscences.

Years later I remembered my mother's silence and I wondered about it. What had it really been like to grow up in that house? However, at the time my aunt actually told these stories, the question of whether they were true or not did not even enter my mind. The distance between them and our room with its kerosene lamp was the measure of my enchantment.

These stories made me see my aunt and my mother as two people who were strange and quite different from me. Of course their physical presence was as I had always known it, and it continued to be familiar and dear to me. Beyond it, however, I could now visualize a whole realm of people and their settings, which were part of them but which I would never know.

Without knowing what I was feeling, I experienced at this time the sadness that comes with the awareness of the limited knowledge we have even of those with whom we are most intimate. Just as they would never know the world that I would inhabit one day as an adult, the early part of their lives would remain to me forever a mystery. The glimpse of the past that I caught through my aunt's stories continued to intrigue me with what it concealed as well as with what it revealed.

III

ANOTHER STORY. ANOTHER time. A different setting. It's late afternoon and my aunt is sitting with me in the kitchen. A thick, savoury soup is simmering. My aunt lets me taste it for her. Once again I feel physically disoriented. I can smell the soup, hear the voices of our neighbours, feel my hunger before the food. Yet, I sense these are false clues. My senses are betraying me. When my aunt resumes her story my confusion fades.

We are back in the pre-war world. I have only to step through our door, run down the stairs into the street, and I will find Dobryd before its destruction. I will walk through it with a sense of familiarity, its plan etched in my mind by my aunt's words.

"When I was a child we lived in the country house most of the year. I remember whenever we came to Dobryd I thought it large and splendid.

"Then, at the age of fourteen, I was sent to boarding school in Vienna. Your grandfather, who felt at home in most of the capitals of Europe, wanted his children to know something of life beyond Dobryd. It was my first time away from home, and I realized that Dobryd was, after all, only a small town.

"But it was never *just* a small town. Perhaps the fact of being near the renowned University of Lwow had something to do with it. There was also a tradition in the area that the people of Dobryd were a special breed. Wherever they might emigrate, they always distinguished themselves in some way. In any case, there was never anything sleepy or dull about the place, nor about the life that went on in your grandfather's house.

"When I first arrived at school, I remember that my teachers were surprised to find that I was as accomplished as any of the other students in the kind of knowledge that was then considered essential for a young girl. I spoke German as well as they did, my handwriting was sufficiently beautiful to hold up as an example, I had studied the violin, and I knew every variety of handiwork that was fashionable. I was also very skilful in making my own designs which the other girls copied.

"At first when I arrived no one had ever heard of Dobryd. The first year I brought two of my new friends home for the holidays. Our house was always full of young people. Your grandfather enjoyed having them. He always said that he had more in common with them than with people his own age. It was very lively and gay during the holidays. My friends were surprised to find such charming, well-informed people in a place they had never even heard about. When we were back in school, they told the others about their visit, and from then on I was no longer teased about being homesick.

"Many years later, when your uncle was wounded in Italy during World War I, I went to keep him company while he convalesced. The hospital was in Naples and as soon as he was better we did a lot of sightseeing together. One time we spent a whole day in Pompeii. I was astonished by the level of civilization people had enjoyed there before its destruction. I had no sense of foreboding then, yet somehow it reminded me of Dobryd—a small town, distant from the centre of the world, Rome in this case, yet enjoying a rich and complex culture. By comparison, the villages we had passed that morning seemed to belong to a much more primitive epoch.

"Although we lived in the country until your mother was born, most of your grandfather's family lived in

Dobryd. Your grandfather was born there, and his family had lived there for as long as anyone could remember. In every generation there were always some who left. The younger ones went to study abroad, in Vienna or Lausanne. Often they would settle there. Others emigrated to New York or Montevideo, not out of choice, but because of some scandal or a sudden bankruptcy. I remember that these cousins cried when they came to say good-bye to us. How we pitied them.

"Often they became prosperous in their new homes. Some of their new wealth was spent on trips to Dobryd and lavish presents. Yet we always sympathized with them for having to live out their lives amongst strangers. Their sons and daughters, born and raised in distant cities, were also sent home on holidays to acquaint them with the rest of the family. Their parents secretly hoped that when they returned they would bring back a bride or a future husband. This was only one of the ways in which the links between Dobryd and other faraway places were constantly renewed and strengthened.

"One regular visitor from abroad was your great-uncle Louis. I don't think you ever saw him. No, of course you couldn't have. He came for the last time just before you were born and after that there was no way for him to return. He's probably still alive. After all, it's only been six years and he was a vigorous, elegant man, who seemed years younger than his age.

"He was your grandfather's younger brother, always eager to travel and to experience life beyond the family circle. He decided to emigrate to the United States. His parents wept and argued and mourned for him as if he had contracted a fatal illness. In the end when they realized he would not be swayed, they equipped him with money and letters of introduction, and he promised to return and visit them often. But in America, he was too restless to remain in one place. He kept on travelling across the country until he reached California, and after a few months he resumed his journey. I was only a child then, but I remember the excitement in our house whenever a postcard arrived from him. After everyone had read it I was allowed to save it, and your uncle got the postage stamp for his collection.

"Eventually he settled in Louisiana, probably because it was as different as could be from his native region. To everyone's surprise he became in time a very prosperous cotton mill owner. He still wrote often, and even after his parents were dead he continued to come to Dobryd once a year. During these visits he behaved like the proverbial rich uncle from America, showering everyone with extravagant presents and leaving us children with our mouths open while he told us of his adventures. We adored him of course. At the end of his stay he would always try to persuade one of us to visit with him for a while. We would have gone readily, but of course your grandmother wouldn't hear of it. To her, America was a land of savages, paupers and criminals, and she wouldn't let her children have anything to do with such people.

"In 1938 he visited Dobryd for the last time, bringing with him tickets and visas for our entire family. He was deeply worried about what the Germans might do under Hitler. Yet he couldn't convince any of us to leave. Now, of course, our attitude seems insane. But then, you see, we had our families, our involvements, friends, positions, land that we valued. Mostly, I suppose, we felt safe. After all, ours was by no means

a peaceful region. There had been wars before and
we had survived. We were so much a part of Poland
it was impossible to imagine the kind of betrayal that
was being prepared all around us.

"Uncle Louis left alone, with his useless visas, and
the last letter we received from him urged us one
final time to get away from Dobryd. By then it was
already too late.

"Well, let's not talk about those sad times. I want
to tell you about Dobryd as it was before the war.

"The one place that symbolized Dobryd for me was
the Café Imperiale. Everybody went there. It was the
town's most fashionable meeting place, the heart of
its social life, located on the promenade that led from
the public gardens to the town's main square.

"You and I have walked that street many times
together, but of course nothing remains of its former
splendour. Do you remember the tree stumps that
we passed every ten yards or so? These were once
tall chestnut trees. Beneath them children played, parents exchanged greetings with friends, young people
courted and fell in love. The trees were as old as
the town. The Germans cut them down to use as
firewood.

"On a Sunday afternoon everyone was to be found
along the promenade. People came to see and to be
seen. The ladies examined each other with great care.
They dressed in their best clothes and there were
costumes there that would not have been out of place
in Paris or Berlin. The ladies of Dobryd subscribed
to fashion magazines from the big cities and as soon
as they arrived, dressmakers would be set to work,
copying the photographs. In another week or so these
accurate and exquisitely made reproductions were
being admired during the Sunday promenade.

"Sometimes during the Sunday walk, people would stop for refreshments in one of the several cafés along the way. The Café Imperiale was the most elegant and popular of these meeting places. The walls were of black marble, illuminated by bracketed candelabra. The tables were marble as well, and around them were armchairs of deep red velour. The adults usually ordered strong coffee which would arrive with a thick coating of cream. For the children there were delicate, chiffon-light pastries with cream fillings, and coloured ices. Everyone drank mineral water, which was always served with small crystal plates of fruit preserves. Dear God, just talking about it makes my mouth water."

My aunt stops. It is getting dark, but I guess that her eyes are filled with tears. I don't press her to go on. I know that sooner or later she will return to the story on her own. She is as caught up in it as I am. We both sense it is best to break off before my mother and Yuri come home. Their disapproval spoils our pleasure and so we try to keep our pastime secret.

Sometimes, however, my mother noticed that my aunt had been crying. She would be angry and scold both of us. She would take me aside and tell me that I mustn't ask for stories constantly, that it wasn't good for my aunt to live in the past so much. But I didn't believe her. I knew how my aunt's face changed when she told her stories. How young and proud and gay she looked for the time that the story lasted. The next day, when she started where we left off, we returned to the past with the urgency and pleasure derived from forbidden pastimes.

IV

MY AUNT AND I are seated in her kiosk. It is early in the morning and there are few customers. We have all the time in the world to continue the story of Dobryd. There is a small stove in the corner and we sit close to it for the warmth. Occasionally we fill our cups with tea from the kettle that we keep hot all day. When someone comes to visit my aunt, they will take my place next to her and I will run off to look for my friends. For the moment, however, we are alone together, separated from the rest of the marketplace by the images my aunt evokes for us.

"I told you that Dobryd was never a dull or sleepy place. Whatever was happening in the big capitals sooner or later found its echo in Dobryd. Good and bad, it all came here. The young people of the town adopted ideas that were fashionable with young people everywhere at that time.

"I remember when the anarchists were in the news in Vienna and Berlin; Dobryd too had its little band of zealous followers.

"Who were they? Well, mostly they were idle young men, rebelling against their fathers by pretending to challenge all order. I remember they marched a lot and they carried a huge black flag. Occasionally they would get into fist-fights with the police, but mostly they were a nuisance rather than a serious menace. Once however, one of their pranks got out of hand.

There was a bomb and some people were injured. It was written up in the Warsaw *Gazette*.

"Psychoanalysis was becoming fashionable then as well. One of the town's brightest young men went off to Vienna to study with the master. We all read about it. I understood little of what I read, and even that seemed highly outrageous to me, but I tended to side with those who were most enthusiastic. The students in Dobryd were divided into two groups: the followers of Freud and the followers of Marx. Of the two I preferred the first group, perhaps because your mother and her friends belonged to the other side. I found them humorless and very naïve. In our group it seemed to me we were closer to reality and we enjoyed ourselves more. In any case, the ideas, the books were there and we brought to them the same passion that kept young people awake late into the night in all the large European cities.

"There was also a feminist movement but for some reason they were taken even less seriously than the anarchists. They had their own special dedicated following, but the rest of the town laughed at them. Why? I don't know really. They were just considered ridiculous and that was that.

"Their leader was an American girl, Maria. She had come to the town on a visit with her parents. One of our doctors had fallen in love with her and she married him and remained in Dobryd. Your poor aunt Celia was her friend and that's how we all got to know her. She was a lovely woman and somehow no one ever laughed at her, even if they laughed at the marches she organized, and at some of her other activities. Your mother was a little girl then and she would often follow Celia on these marches. When they noticed her they would send her to the head of the column. Your mother enjoyed this a great deal, until your grandmother heard about it and put a quick stop to her activities. Once she was older she immediately joined the movement just to spite your grandmother. After all, your grandfather had always encouraged his daughters as much as his son. He was an exception in his time and his class.

"I want to tell you about Maria, so you will remember her. She should never be forgotten. She was young when she took up the feminist cause. No one could understand why she chose to make herself ridiculous. Being the wife of a small town doctor had a lot to do with it. The poorer Jewish women in the ghettos, you see, were really miserable creatures—they were considered inferior from birth. When they married, their wishes were rarely consulted. They had many children whom they usually had to provide for by taking in work or keeping shop while their husbands spent their days praying and studying the holy books. Even on feast days they had to serve their husbands and sons first, and they were not allowed to sit next to them in the synagogue.

"The conditions of the Christian women who came to see her husband were even worse. Most of the time they were the only beasts of burden their husbands could afford. A Polish peasant usually wore out two or three in his lifetime.

"Unfortunately, the women Maria wanted most to reach were the ones who, under their husbands' orders, closed their doors in her face. Her following consisted of a small number of enlightened, middle-class women, like your aunt Celia, for whom feminism was another way of being 'modern' and filling their days.

"Yet Maria was never discouraged. Always full of

energy, she rushed about town from morning till
night, seeing to her women, organizing volunteers,
giving of herself to anyone who needed her. At the
end of her life, when she was in her forties, it was
reported that she had retained her spirit of defiance
and her courage.

"It happened in Treblinka. I wish you might never
know of such places, but from now on all children
will be taught about them. That way it may never
happen again. Treblinka was a place where people
were taken to be killed. Many people from our town
died there and often they did not suspect what was
going to happen to them until it was actually happening. This was a horror without precedent, and the
worst rumours tended to be discounted. We refused
to believe what we heard.

"Maria was taken to Treblinka with her husband,
but they were separated as soon as they arrived. A
few hours later she found herself surrounded by a
group of women all of them naked and shivering,
their heads shaved, waiting to go into the "showers"
from which they would never come out alive. In the
few minutes that remained before the doors opened
for them, Maria had somehow guessed the sinister
purpose of those showers. She passed the word along
to her companions. It was the last time that she was
to appeal to them and they did not let her down.
When the moment came and the guards were moving
the women along, Maria's group turned on the guards
and attacked them. The guards were armed and the
women had only their teeth and nails to use against
them, but they fought fiercely. Somehow the story
survived them. It spread throughout the camp and
beyond it. I heard about it almost as soon as we
returned to Dobryd. You must never forget it. Maria

was a heroine, a true heroine of Dobryd, and she was not the only one."

Our first interruption. A customer waits to be served, but for once I don't mind the intrusion. My aunt's words are ringing in my ears, my heart feels heavy and my head hurts. I feel as if I am being crushed by a terrible weight. I want to get away from it and ease the pain that almost paralyses me. I make my way out of the kiosk and for a while I wander about the marketplace. All my usual pleasures are there but this morning there is no comfort in them. Almost in spite of myself I make my way back to my aunt.

V

MY AUNT IS alone once again. There is a fresh glass of tea in her hands, and as soon as she sees me approach she rises to prepare one for me. With it there is a plate of my favourite cookies. The warm liquid is very soothing. I sip it slowly, waiting patiently for my aunt to begin.

Instead, however, she turns to me and takes my face in her hands. "You don't look well, my child. Are you all right? Perhaps your mother is right. These stories aren't good for you. I must stop talking to you this way. You know, sometimes I forget how old you are. I even forget you're here and God knows what you're thinking all this time."

I try to reassure her: "I'm fine, *ciociu*. Really, my friends tell me even worse stories about the war. Everybody hears them at home. But I want to hear them from you."

These exchanges are part of the storytelling ritual. We know, even as my aunt protests and I reassure her, that sooner or later we will give way to our usual pastime—our secret vice that separates us from everyone else.

"Dobryd. Yes, we were talking of Dobryd. Its young people. How fine they seem to me now. They were filled with a kind of naïve idealism that glowed in them and transformed them. Of course it was the age of idealism, of new ideas. We believed the world could be changed. We quarrelled about methods, and each group thought the other mistaken, but we were all united in our belief that a better world was coming and we would make it. The most unlikely people became the most ardent revolutionaries.

"I'm thinking of Grisha, a friend of your mother's, but first I have to tell you something about the communists of that time. Yes, I know you've heard that word from Yuri, but the young people I'm thinking of were quite different from Yuri and his friends. The ones I knew spent most of their time on the terrace of the Café Imperiale. There they sat, day after day, talking, arguing. Some of them were your mother's close friends. They formed a study group, and together they immersed themselves in the works of Hegel, Marx, Lenin.

"When you're older perhaps your mother will tell you more about these men. In any case the young communists of Dobryd were for the most part content to argue about texts. Just as their fathers and grandfathers a generation back had spent their days in prayer houses studying and interpreting the sacred books.

"However, a few young people did more than just argue and talk. Instead of waiting for the new order to come to them they set out to seek it, to make it happen.

"I want to tell you about two of these people because they were special friends of your mother's. Grisha and Halka.

"Grisha was the son of one of the town's richest and most respected families. As an only child, delicate from birth, he had been cherished and over-protected. He was an intelligent and curious boy, and his father spared no effort to provide him with the best tutors and the latest books. Somehow, the new ideas that were then so much in the wind reached this sheltered adolescent and found their mark. Alone in his room, without any inspiration or guidance other than his books and journals, knowing very little about life outside his home, he became a revolutionary.

"The only real revolution around then was the one that had taken place in Russia and so Grisha began preparations for making his way there. While everyone around him fussed and worried about his health, he was plotting a course of action that was to remove him from all luxury and protection and lead him to the heart of revolutionary activity. He was very ingenious about it. I can't imagine how he managed to keep his activities secret from a family as close as his.

"I remember him very well. Occasionally he would have dinner with us. A pale, thin boy, very serious and yet also childlike, like someone who had only learned about life from books. To us, his disappearance seemed even more shocking than to the rest of the town.

"A few weeks before his twentieth birthday he vanished from Dobryd. His parents spared no effort to find him, but the weeks went by and there was no hint or trace of his whereabouts. The whole town was rife with speculation. The boy's parents came to see your mother and beseeched her to tell them anything she might know. But she knew no more than anyone else. It was true that she had been Grisha's friend but they had never really been close. Grisha was already then exercising the discipline of a revolutionary and he kept his plans to himself.

All sorts of rumours began to spread about him. There was talk in the town of spirits, enchantments, spells. The parents were desperate enough to pursue the most far-fetched clues but it was useless.

"Then he himself resolved the mystery. A letter from him, postmarked in the Soviet Union, arrived at his parents' house. He told them that they must forget about him. From now on he would only live to bring about the revolution where it was most needed. The pain he caused his parents, he wrote, was insignificant compared to the misery most people lived in. They must find comfort in the fact that he was now happier than he had ever been.

"Grisha was true to his word. The letter was the only communication ever received from him. But they heard about him indirectly, and through constant inquiry they kept up with the events of his life. He was frequently imprisoned in different European cities where the Party sent him as an organizer. He seemed to turn up whenever a strike or an uprising occurred. Eventually he became quite important in

the Party. Your mother heard that he had been sent
on a diplomatic mission to Germany.

"I can't even imagine him in all those roles. I wonder
if he survived the war? His parents were among the
first killed. They could have bought their way out.
They had enough money, and at that time it could
still be done, but they seemed to have lost their desire
to live. Who knows, Grisha may even turn up here
one day looking for them."

My aunt stops for a minute's rest. We both look about
us as if we expect Grisha to step forth from amongst
the shoppers in the marketplace and identify himself
to us. His story horrifies me. I cannot bear to hear
of the cruelty he has shown his parents. I think of
myself and my aunt and my mother and I promise
myself that I will never leave them, not even when
I'm grown up. I will never make them cry. Impulsively,
I rush over to my aunt and wrap my arms around
her and press against her with all my might.

She looks surprised, and then pleased, and hugs
me to her.

VI

MY AUNT AND I are walking home from the market.
The ruins we pass have become the familiar landscape
of my childhood and I no longer see them. But then
my aunt draws my attention to a particular spot:

"Your mother's friend Halka lived right over there.

It was one of the grandest houses in Dobryd. That stone lion is all that's left. I remember there were two of them. They stood like sentries on either side of the door that led into the inner courtyard.

"Halka was your mother's closest friend. When you were born, it was already war time, but Halka managed to make her way from Paris to Dobryd to see your mother and have a look at you. It was a mad thing to do, since there was a good chance that she would never make it back to Paris. She was wild and strong-willed and very courageous.

"Your mother and she became friends in secondary school. But we all knew of her long before your mother brought her home. Her father was the town's richest citizen as well as its meanest. He was a widower with four children, of whom Halka was the youngest. It was said in the town that the children might as well have been total orphans for all the attention their father gave them. When he remarried he chose a woman who shared his passion for money. Halka, like her sisters and brothers, grew up neglected, but of all the children she was treated most harshly because of her rebellious spirit.

"As a child she often ran away from home, and her capture would always be followed by a humiliating walk through the streets of the town with her father holding her by her collar. Everyone in the town pitied her but since they all feared her father, no one intervened. After she became friends with your mother, our parents, knowing her situation at home, practically adopted her. She was constantly with us, and for your mother she became more of a sister than either I or Celia ever were. They were the same age and had many ideas in common. They often closed themselves off from the rest of us in that secret world they shared.

"Sometime during one of those long conversations of theirs, Halka must have told your mother of a discovery she had made and what she planned to do with it.

"Since childhood she had heard the stories everyone in the town told of her father's enormous wealth. She herself had never seen any of it, nor did she ever benefit from it. When it came to money her father regarded his children with the same suspicion as his servants, convinced that everyone was conspiring to rob him. He was really quite mad.

"Halka began spying on him. At first she did it without any special motive, simply for spite. When the tenants came to pay their rents she would watch them and her father from some hidden corner. The house which she hated and from which she had always fled at every opportunity now began to fascinate her. She was convinced that the secret she sought to discover was to be found within its walls.

"I learned all this many years later. In those long nights in the loft, when we could not sleep because of cold and hunger, your mother and I became closer than we had ever been before the war. It was during these sleepless nights that she talked to me of Halka.

"I had only once been inside Halka's home, but it was the sort of place I would never forget. It was immense, silent and secret, the kind of house that figured in the mystery stories I loved as a young girl. I had no trouble fitting Halka's story against this background.

"She haunted the house like the ghosts the peasants claimed they saw emerging from it on moonlit nights.

Eventually her persistence paid off. She discovered that the large trunks in which the household linen and eiderdown were stored were lined with false bottoms and double sides. Inside these, her father kept his money. Each room of the large house contained several of these trunks lined in gold coin. They were always locked and the keys belonged to her father, but in a brief interval when her father lay unconscious in bed because of an illness, she managed to secure the keys and have them copied.

My aunt stops for a minute to catch her breath. I'm spellbound by her words and I can't wait.

"Go on. What happened? What happened then?"

But she has a natural bent for the storyteller's tyranny. Her pauses, like her digressions, are part of the master plan. My eagerness is kindled, and then momentarily denied, so that the ultimate pleasure may be the most potent possible.

"All right. Well, as I said, after so many weeks of watching and waiting, Halka was now in possession of the information that had become her sole preoccupation. But what was she to do with it? This was something that had not occurred to her before. For some time she did nothing at all, satisfied with the mere knowledge of the powerful weapon she now possessed against her father.

"After a while, an idea of what to do with the money crystallized itself and she was propelled out of her passive contentment into a new round of activity.

"Halka belonged to a secret communist youth group, made up of other students from the gymnasium which she and your mother attended. The group was directed by one of their teachers. Most of the other students belonged to the group because of the usual adolescent taste for secret societies, special languages and codes which separated them from the adult world. But Halka and a few other students were serious revolutionaries. They considered discussions an indulgence of intellectuals. They scorned the usual occupations of their class, as well as all work which did not require manual labour. In preparation for the new life they were to lead one day, they were learning the trades and skills they thought they would need.

"I remember, it was about this time that your mother, who had so far frustrated all your grandmother's attempts to introduce her to the processes involved in running a household, suddenly began to show the keenest interest in the very activities that she had always scorned. Your grandmother was pleased because she had always hoped your rebellious mother would one day find the same contentments as other women of her class. She would still not go near an embroidery needle or participate in your grandmother's afternoon teas, but it was sufficiently miraculous to all of us that she even ventured into the kitchen. She kept her distance from the rest of us, but she began to follow the servants while they went about their work. She was so persistent and serious that after first laughing at her, the servants began to complain that she made them uneasy.

"What none of us knew, of course, was that your mother was learning about the "real" world, as she had been instructed to do. The ultimate goal of all this mysterious activity was a settlement that had been founded a few years back in the Palestinian desert by a previous cell from the gymnasium. Here the sons and daughters of the middle class, destined for the

80

occupations of their fathers and mothers, lived communally, working as shepherds, farmers, bricklayers, striving to make themselves self-sufficient under incredibly difficult conditions. At the same time they were carrying on a fight against British rule and local landowners. It was an existence that combined their dual ideals of revitalizing the land and organizing the Arabs and immigrants to fight the "bosses".

"I was never a part of this group and I can't tell you much about it. Perhaps your mother will when you are older.

"Well, Halka had always intended to join the settlement. The discovery of her father's money precipitated her date of departure. Now she had not only herself to give to the cause, but also her father's treasure. She would deliver the money from its idleness and force it to serve people who needed it. It had to serve a greater purpose than merely to satisfy her father's madness and greed. At the same time, of course, she would also inflict the cruelest punishment possible on her father for his treatment of her.

"Your mother was taken into Halka's confidence. Together they worked out the details of removing the money gradually and hiding it in your mother's bedroom. When Halka left in the spring of 1935, your mother was the only person in the town who knew that she was on a train heading to Romania, en route to Palestine.

"Her escape was entirely successful but it did not bring about the ruin of the father Halka hated. The loss of a few bags of gold coins hardly made a dent in his fortune. Nor did he seem to suffer from his daughter's betrayal. In fact, he prospered more than ever. It took the Germans to finish him off. Before they killed him, he became as humble and as trembling as those who had lived in fear of him. But even Halka would have found little satisfaction in that.

"What happened to her? We don't know. As I've told you, she returned only once—when you were born. She stayed for two hours, and then disappeared as mysteriously as she came. If she is alive, she will find us again. I'm certain of that. In fact, I'm almost sure she is alive. Who can tell, one day you may even come to know her."

My aunt's last words launch me into a daydream about the past and the present. In it, Dobryd, my great-uncle Louis, Grisha, Halka, my young mother, I, my aunt, the marketplace among the ruins, the Café Imperiale, Yuri and his friends, all coexist without contradiction. My characters circle each other like figures in a dance, grace in their movements. I watch over them. Their emotions and my own flow through me, while I control their gestures by transposing my own longings and desires into their existence.

VII

MANY YEARS LATER, after I thought I had forgotten the stories that my aunt had told, as one forgets childhood pastimes, I continued to come in contact with events and people who revived these stories and added new or final chapters to them. They insisted on being remembered, and eventually the threads of these stories became entangled with those of my own life.

A year or so after the war, we learned that my great-uncle Louis, my grandfather's brother, had died in Louisiana without seeing Germany defeated. Even in those dark years he could not believe that the war would mean the end of Dobryd or its people. But his anger at their blind stubbornness in the face of his warnings affected his feelings towards the place. In his will he specified that his estate was to be used to help the survivors of Dobryd make new lives for themselves elsewhere. Nothing was to go to those who chose to remain in Poland.

My mother and my aunt, at the time when they needed his help most, must often have regretted my uncle's wishes. In the end, however, it turned out as he had foreseen. Life in that haunted landscape became too painful for them to endure any longer and they decided to leave Poland. It was then that my uncle's legacy finally helped them as he had anticipated all along.

At about the same time as we learned of my great-uncle's death, Grisha reappeared in Dobryd, just as my aunt had predicted he would. One day as my aunt and I returned from the marketplace we were surprised to see my mother deep in conversation with a strange man. He wore an army uniform, but it was not anyone I had ever seen before. My aunt did not recognize him, even when he came towards her and embraced her with great feeling. My mother pronounced the name, and my aunt and I both stood lost in amazement. My aunt, I suppose, because she could not find any trace of the quiet, frail adolescent she had known in this robust soldier, while I was overwhelmed by the implications that Grisha's presence had for me: it became apparent, for the first time, that the world of my aunt's stories might have indeed existed once.

Grisha, on his way west with his regiment, had

stopped off in Dobryd to learn the fate of his parents. My mother had already told him of their death, and this news reawakened in him some long-buried nostalgia for the world he had rejected. My mother and he talked late into the night. Several times when I woke up, I heard their voices. In the morning he was gone.

My mother and Grisha corresponded from then on, and they even met once again some years later. It happened while my mother was visiting Halka in Paris. Grisha was there as a delegate to some international congress. My mother, when she returned, told us the meeting had not been a very happy one. For one thing there was a great political schism between them now. My mother had left Poland, disillusioned, to live in a capitalist country. Grisha would not accept her reasons for this move, and in the end they separated estranged. After this meeting their correspondence was reduced to a few cards, and eventually it ceased altogether. Just recently I came across his name in a list of imprisoned Soviet citizens of Jewish origin published in a local newspaper. The list had been handed to the Russian ambassador to Canada by a group of concerned Canadian citizens.

Halka reappeared in our lives after we had already left Poland. We were living in Montreal when Halka's first letter reached us. It had been travelling a long time and it had followed us to all the places we had passed through since the end of the war. At last it caught up with us in Canada. My mother had made inquiries about Halka but with less success. The last news she had of her was that she had been deported from Palestine with the young French communist whom she had married, and that they now lived somewhere in France. When the war came along, Halka and her husband had been active in the Resistance and that was the last my mother heard of them. She feared the worst.

She was deeply affected by Halka's letter. Her solid, stoic manner, so characteristic of her during those early difficult years in Canada, gave way. She became a softer, warmer person. The letter had a significance beyond its content. In finding Halka she had found an eye-witness to what her own life had once been like, and the kind of person she had been. For a short while she recovered her lost self.

Halka was now living in Paris with her husband and two children. My mother went over to see them. She had many stories to tell when she returned and her dearest wish, she said, was that one day I would come to know her friend.

Some ten years later I went to Paris as a student. I looked up Halka and her family and liked them all immediately. I began to spend a lot of time with them and they became my special guides to France.

One day, a rare sunny Sunday, we drove out to Senlis to visit its ancient cathedral. In the afternoon, after a long picnic lunch, we decided to walk along the ramparts that surrounded the town. After a while we stopped to enjoy the sun on a stone bench facing the town. It was then that Halka first spoke of Dobryd to me. In all the months that I had been coming to her house she had never mentioned it, and I had been so preoccupied with my new life in Paris that the thought of Dobryd had been very distant.

She seemed as surprised as I when she mentioned its name. Her memories of Dobryd, she told me, had never been very pleasant, and with time she had almost forgotten it. Suddenly, perhaps because of my presence, our walk along the ramparts had aroused in her a flood of images that she had not recalled in years.

Dobryd, like Senlis, had been a walled town. Its ramparts dated from medieval times, but unlike those near us, which had been preserved and treasured, they had been neglected and were crumbling. In Dobryd the ramparts were mostly sought out by young couples who came there for shelter and privacy. In amazing detail Halka described to me and to her husband a place she had not seen in years—the walls, their footpaths, the stone seats, similar to the one we sat on, the abandoned cannon, left over from a forgotten war but now only a prop for children's games, and all the secret little openings and paths that occurred along the meandering circumference of the walls. As she spoke, those walls of memory seemed to merge with the ramparts we sat on, and the Plain of France could as easily have been the fields of Galicia.

I never heard Halka speak of Dobryd again and I never thought of her in terms of it. It was only when I returned to Montreal and noticed how alike Halka and my mother were in so many ways, that I realized how much of their resemblance had its source in Dobryd. A small, insignificant town had marked them so indelibly that to me they would always seem set apart from other people.

Was Dobryd really unique, as it had always seemed to me? Can I trust its portrait rendered in nostalgia? The place no longer exists, not even in name. The Russians renamed it after they annexed and rebuilt it. It seems appropriate to me that like other lost cities, it has left behind it only a mythical legacy that goes beyond fact.

PART FOUR

I

A SHORT TIME after my mother began working for the Russians as a translator, she received a bonus for her work which made her the envy of our neighbours. The night she brought it home—a small piece of paper with her photograph attached, permitting her to travel anywhere in Poland—she, Yuri and my aunt talked of nothing else. It was hard for me to share their excitement. All I understood from their conversation was that my mother could now travel as often as she liked and that she would have to be very careful.

Why should she want to leave Dobryd, I wondered. The prospect of my mother's travels did not please me at all. I dreaded being separated from her for any length of time. Fear entered my heart. What if something terrible happened to her on one of her journeys and she never returned?

Later that night, when my mother came into my room, my anxiety spilled over. She smiled and reassured me. She promised she would never be gone very long, not more than a day or so. There was no danger at all. At the end of her trips there would always be a gift for me.

I trusted her and my fears retreated.

She soon began going regularly to Lwow, the old
university town some ninety kilometres west of Dobryd. At the end of the war it had quickly re-established
its claim to being the most important city in the region.
The university had been reduced to ruins, but its
marketplace, the criterion of civilization in those days,
was already renowned. Sitting in my aunt's booth,
I had often heard travellers extol its merits. These
descriptions roused my curiosity and reconciled me
to my mother's departures.

In our family, the trips became the highlight of
the week. The rest of the time we either helped my
mother prepare for one, or we listened to her tell
us what she had seen and heard during her absence.
The nights when she was to return from Lwow I
insisted on waiting up for her no matter how late
it was, and my aunt, for once, thought of something
other than my well-being. Together we would wait,
for the moment contemporaries, since in contrast to
my mother, we were both helpless, weak children.

I didn't know why my mother went to Lwow every
week, nor how she managed to bring back the things
she did. She returned flushed, tired, but always
triumphant, her arms full of packages—surprises for
me and my aunt. When she talked of her trips I understood only bits and pieces of what she said, yet I loved
to listen to her and watch her face as she recreated
her day for us.

What enchanted me most about those trips, more
than the things she brought back for me, was the
effect the trips had on her and consequently on us.
My mother was then in her early thirties. The war
had marked her, as it had everyone else. She had
lost her husband, parents, a brother, sisters, most of
her friends. The war had destroyed her home, a way

of life, the beliefs that had been the core of her existence. It left her physically ravaged—her weight had been halved during the two and a half years we lay hidden in the barn loft. Now she had to provide for us in a world that was as alien as anything could possibly be to the enlightened, prosperous milieu in which she had spent most of her life.

Yet in spite of what she had endured, there was nothing passive or submissive about her. People always thought of her as someone very strong, someone to lean on in difficulties, a person who seemed in charge of her life.

I had absolute faith in her. I knew she would take care of me and that with her I was always safe. The events of my childhood, terrible as they were, did not affect me as might be expected. My mother was always there, a protective barrier between me and all evil. Because of her presence and her strength, I grew up with the impression that mine had been a happy childhood. Strange as it seems, this was how I always thought of it.

As a child I was never taken into her confidence, and I knew very little of what she thought or felt. When I compare her with the other adults I knew, she stands in my memory apart from them, illuminated by the energy and vitality that always emanated from her. In those days everyone who came near her seemed to me by comparison half-dead and because I belonged to her, I knew that nothing really terrible would happen to me.

Somehow she left me and others with the impression that even during the war and immediately after it she did more than just survive. There was a sense of satisfaction about her life then. She had fought against impossible odds and won. Years later, in

Canada, living in prosperity and peace, her sense of resolution and strength ebbed away. As I grew older I became familiar with her frailties and her limitations, but the impression from my childhood remained with me despite all the changes in her and in me.

On the days she returned safely from Lwow, it was as if a spark had reanimated all of us. My aunt forgot her burden of grief and rejoiced, restored to the vital person she must once have been. At these moments, I could picture her as the young lady of her stories. The rest of the time she was as the war had made her —a frightened, superstitious woman, ageless and old at the same time. The simplest acts of everyday life had become terrifying obstacles for her, and she turned more and more to omens, old wives' tales and the magic of repetition to help her through her days. I sensed even then that my aunt had lost touch with reality, but it was only much later that I became familiar with the terrifying world she inhabited.

Yet, on the nights when my mother was about to return and my aunt was busy cooking for her, I would look at her and see, not someone familiar, but someone whom I regretted not knowing. I would have given anything to keep my aunt as she was just then, smiling, animated, in control.

When my mother finally arrived, we both rushed at her, filled with excitement. Sometimes it seemed to me that my aunt was the true child in these moments. It was something about the way she would lose herself totally in the pleasure of my mother's return, while I viewed them both from a certain distance.

I watched my aunt. Her eyes turned an intense blue, the fair skin of her face flushed, her hands, always occupied, seemed suddenly fragile and fluttering. Surreptitiously, because she knew my mother disapproved of this habit, she lit a candle in the corner of the room, an offering for my mother's safe return. In a few minutes, the emotions that caused this transformation subsided and she became her familiar self once again.

After my mother had been going to Lwow for some time, I became dissatisfied with waiting for her, receiving my present, and listening to her adventures. I wanted to go with her. My pleading to take me along became a ritual of her departures. She always refused, of course, and her reasons were valid enough to satisfy any adult: the roads were bad, the trucks that picked her up were crowded and would not stop for a woman with a child, she wanted to keep me away from large crowds. But to a child, they meant nothing. There had to be something else. I was certain she was keeping the real reason from me.

Perhaps I had caught this habit of suspicion from my aunt, who was never satisfied with the explanations that seemed plausible to most people. As it happened I was right to doubt my mother. But there was no satisfaction in my discovery.

I learned the truth about my mother's trips from Elsa, the daughter of one of our neighbours. It was on a day that had begun with much pleasure. I had a new dress, my first real dress. Until then my aunt had made my clothes from old remnants or dyed sackcloth.

Elsa was one of those girls who are born to be coquettes. There was no other way of explaining her obsession with her appearance. She did not acquire her tastes from her grandmother, with whom she lived. Nor were there any women at the time in the town whom Elsa could have regarded as models to emulate. Yet, in spite of the drabness around us, Elsa, on the verge of adolescence, managed to develop the same preoccupations with grooming that I was to discover a few years later among teenagers in Canada. When I came down the stairs from our flat, I spotted her in the doorway leading to the courtyard, but I didn't go over to her. Normally she had no use for me: I was much too young to share her pastimes or to be of any interest to her. This time, however, my changed appearance roused her. She called me over and I walked towards her, proud of her attention, and stiff with the responsibility of keeping my new clothes clean. Elsa looked me over with enthusiasm.

"How nice you look!" she exclaimed. "I wish I could get something decent to wear." An expression of resentment and spite settled over her pretty features. "You're lucky. Your mother works for the Russians and she can get you anything you want."

"You're wrong," I protested. "My mother didn't get this dress from the Russians. She bought it for me in Lwow."

Elsa looked at me with contempt. "I know how she got it better than you do, silly. Of course the Russians didn't give it to her. What do you take me for? I'm not a baby like you. I know how much they pay. But I also know that she didn't just buy it. She must have stolen plenty from the Russians to get that dress for you."

For a long moment I could think of nothing to say. Was Elsa serious, or was this just another form of the teasing to which she subjected all those younger than her?

"Stolen? How can you say that? My mother told

me. She said it was just luck. She found someone who needed the money and she bought it for very little."

"You're just a kid. What do you expect her to say? She's not going to tell you the truth. It's too serious a matter for her to trust you with."

At this point Elsa's insinuations clicked with my own previous suspicions. I became certain that she did know something I didn't know. A wave of terror, something like nausea, came over me, and I knew I shouldn't persist. But it was too late. Too much had already been said to turn back.

"What do you know? Tell me. What do you mean—the truth?"

Elsa looked at me in a different way, calculating just how much she could benefit from the anxiety she had just evoked in me. After a minute she turned away, as if she had no further interest in talking to me.

"I can't tell you. I overheard my grandmother talking about it to a neighbour. She'd beat me if she found out I told you. You'd better go away."

But I was not going to be dismissed. Besides, I sensed that Elsa was after something. If only I could guess what it was.

"Your grandmother won't find out. I promise. Look, I'll give you my piece of white tulle. Maybe you can make something out of it." I trembled inside as I committed the precious bit of cloth that wasn't mine to give. But Elsa wasn't interested.

"Don't be stupid. What would I do with that piece of rag? It may be all right for you and my sister and that kid you play with, but don't expect me to play games like that. I'm going to get some proper clothes."

My mind did a quick inventory of all my possessions.

Did I own anything that Elsa would consider fit to wear? All I could think of were some hair ribbons, but surely Elsa would find these too childish as well. I was about to give up in despair, when Elsa herself came up with a suggestion. She must have paid more attention to our games than we suspected.

"I want your perfume bottle."

I hesitated when Elsa named her price. For the last few days our play-acting props had been enriched by a perfume vial with an atomizer attached to it and a handle decorated with a ragged gold fringe. The perfume had been used up long ago, but its fragrance still lingered inside the container. I don't remember which one of us found it. It belonged to the three of us. We kept it at my house, however, along with our other treasures, since we agreed I had the most privacy.

The bottle, like the piece of tulle, was a sacred communal object. By giving it away, wouldn't I be betraying my friends? My heart filled with remorse, but I knew I could not resist Elsa. I ran upstairs, and in a minute the bottle was in my hands. No one saw me with it, and there were no witnesses as I handed it over to Elsa. When she accepted it I felt almost grateful to her. It seemed a small price to pay for the information I was about to receive.

Elsa did not even look at the bottle when I handed it to her, but with a quick, careless gesture she made it disappear.

"What are you going to tell the others?"

"I don't know. I'll make something up."

"Well, that's your worry. Now I'll tell you. My grandmother said your mother steals little bags of sugar from the army storehouse and brings them home, hidden in her clothes. At the end of the week she takes the sugar to Lwow, where she trades it. My grandmother said that what she is doing is very dangerous. If she's caught, they'll shoot her. It's true that everyone steals, and they overlook it if it's an unimportant person, but your mother is the translator for the head colonel. That's an important job. I heard the women say it happened once before. The Russians caught a man who did what your mother does, and shot him on the spot.

"That's all I heard. Now you know how your mother gets all those things for you. Remember, you promised not to tell anyone I told you."

It never occurred to me to doubt Elsa's words. The horror of her explanation fitted in perfectly with the view I myself had of the world—danger lurked everywhere. My pretty new dress carried the price of my mother's life. There were no innocent pleasures.

I had always suspected that my mother and my aunt kept things from me. I knew I was more sheltered than other children. Now it was my turn to keep a secret from them. But how? Where would I find the necessary self-control to hide such terrible knowledge from them?

As I walked away from Elsa, sobs such as I had never experienced convulsed my every step. I made it to our secret shelter. All care for my new dress was forgotten. I saw it now as an object of shame and terror. By wearing it I betrayed my mother to everyone who saw me. I never wanted to put it on again. But how could I explain such an action at home, when only this morning I had been so happy with it?

I stayed in the hideout as long as I could. The degraded condition of my dress seemed to me a proper camouflage. When the crying gave way for a while, it was replaced by grandiose schemes I invented to protect my mother. By the time it became dark outside, I had already given up both alternatives: I was too weak to cry or to hope. Whether my mother continued her trips or not, we were in equal danger. Either way, I was certain we were lost.

I came home later than usual, hoping against all probability that they wouldn't notice me. In fact, just the opposite happened. For once, my mother's anxiety equalled that of my aunt's. My arrival reassured them momentarily, but when they noticed my appearance their fear returned. They fussed over me and tended to me, and then they began to question me.

My tears started again, and with them all my fears came spilling out. I told it all, stumbling over the words, dreading the moment they would be confirmed. My mother heard me out quietly, with attention. When my aunt tried to cut me off with reassurances, she stopped her so I could go on. Then it was her turn to speak. She didn't deny any of it, nor did she offer excuses. Instead she urged me to have confidence in her ability to overcome all odds.

After all, she reminded me, she had escaped from the Germans. Twice they had caught her on the way to the farm where my aunt waited for us, and each time, with me in her arms, she had escaped. She had brought us this far, taking care of our needs where so many others had failed, and she would continue to do so. There was nothing formidable about the Russians. Most of them were young boys, half-starved themselves, one generation away from illiteracy. She wasn't in the least afraid of them. As a matter of fact, most of them were her friends. They respected and liked her. Even if something was discovered, they would cover up for her. I was not to worry. From now on only good things would happen to me.

Did I believe her? She was very convincing. Like all mothers she had magical powers in shaping my perception of reality. I felt comforted and safe as long as she spoke to me. Yet from then on, until some months later when the trips ended, it was impossible for me to participate in the drama my mother and my aunt enacted around her arrivals and departures. I still felt an occasional response, but inside I knew that it was all different than it had been. I now had feelings and thoughts and fears that I had to hide, because I knew that confessing them would only add to my mother's burden. From then on I fully accepted and practised dissimulation and illusion.

It was then, I believe, that I began to develop as a distinct individual, someone other than my mother's child. Like everyone else I was learning to become a private, separate being, aware of parts of myself that I must never expose to others.

II

THE TRIPS TO Lwow stopped when we left Dobryd. Our departure seemed to me a marvellous solution which would remove me from the horror I had experienced since Elsa's revelations. I was overjoyed to leave, even though I had formed many attachments to the ruined city and to my first friends.

Our move came about mostly because of Yuri. Since the day when he and his platoon had liberated us and he had carried me out of the barn into the outside world, we had become his adopted family. When the time came for his regiment to leave Dobryd and move westwards towards Germany, he was not going to leave us behind.

There were other reasons to make us wish to leave Dobryd. Everyone in the town seemed possessed by the need to get away from this unlucky region. There was a frantic scramble for the few daily exit permits. Most people were too impatient to wait out this lengthy and uncertain process, and they chose the quicker route of night-time border crossings. This alternative required not so much courage as money with which to bribe border guards to look the other way. One also had to have a certain unconcern for possessions, since the crossings had to be made on foot with very little encumbrance. This restriction was a serious problem, since people clung to the most useless objects with a tenacity incomprehensible in normal times. Their meagre belongings seemed particularly precious when they were forced to leave them behind.

For some time my family remained apart from all this frenzy. Almost every week another neighbour would come to say good-bye. Yet the possibility of our own departure was not discussed. The reasons that made other people hesitate were not even mentioned in our house. My family lived from day to day, and the future, if it existed for others, no longer held any meaning for us. We excluded ourselves voluntarily from it and looked upon those who did not do so as lacking a sense of decency.

It required a will as strong as Yuri's to force my mother and aunt out of this state. This was a role he had played in our lives from the beginning. From the time we had first come together, he had taken on the task of pulling us slowly and patiently into the world of everyday reality.

The first time I saw him, he himself had seemed outside ordinary limits, a creature from another world. Now he was familiar, and close, part of my everyday world, but I could still remember our first meeting, when I had seen him as an extraordinary, god-like being. At the age of five, I had known only emaciated bodies like my own, for whom the mere act of walking had become almost impossible. In such a setting, Yuri's presence and his appearance could easily pass for something miraculous.

Other things about him confirmed this first vision. In particular, I remember the military decorations he wore. Because of some trick of lighting, they glowed that day with a power of their own. I remained frozen before this marvellous sight, until it came closer and closer and I felt myself lifted into its magical beam.

Yuri was then in his early twenties, tall, with fair hair and a face that was never serious. Like most Russians, he had endured unbelievable hardship and suffering, but their effect on him was not apparent, at least not in the way that ours could be read in our faces and bodies. His enthusiasm and optimism seemed to have shielded him from the worst physical ravages. One had only to listen to Yuri describe the battles he had fought in, to realize how much he felt a part of the eventual success of his country's struggle. His own private interest was insignificant. The common cause was the important one. Physical hardship was also neutralized by the intense camaraderie that existed between him and the other soldiers and the confidence they all shared in their eventual success.

When we first came to know them, at a time when the enemy was beaten and the end was in sight, euphoria had transformed this band of young people into superior beings. Later, when we knew Yuri better, as he came to depend on us for whatever family warmth we could give him, he lost this special aura for me. At times, when he asked my mother's help with the books he was trying to learn from or when he kissed my aunt and thanked her for cooking a favourite dish, or when he gave himself entirely to one of my make-believe games, he seemed to become my contemporary. Still, I never forgot the promise and the beauty he brought with him the first time I saw him. It made the transition from hiding to freedom easier for me in many ways.

I don't know why Yuri was drawn to us more than to the other survivors, perhaps because of me, perhaps because my mother and my aunt were women without men. Yuri was very chivalrous. Although he fought side by side with Russian women soldiers without apparent constraint, with other women his attitude changed. He became very gentle and shy. Towards my aunt, in particular, he behaved with extreme courtesy and refinement. His manner with her seemed somehow incongruous with his usual tough behaviour. He was very appealing.

Yuri's arrival in our lives had seemed miraculous. One day we had been abandoned, starving, without hope. The next day we had acquired a kind and devoted protector. From the very beginning, he had a way of making people laugh, even my mother and my aunt. He was not alone in this. All his friends, the young soldiers he brought with him to visit us, had this characteristic. They had been fighting for months, some of them for years, against terrible odds, yet they had about them an air of gaiety and good cheer. Theirs was the care-free laughter one associates with casual pleasures, and not with fighting and dying.

Soon Yuri began to come to us not only as our protector, but also as a friend. He was delighted with my aunt when she told him to call her *ciociu*, as I did. In a short while, they created a relationship in which she became his distant mother and he was her son who had left for the war. It was an expedient duplication, they realized. They were stand-ins for principals who never appeared. Yet there was genuine feeling between them, apart from the ghosts they sought in each other.

Yuri spoke often of his real mother, whom he hadn't seen or heard from in months. His father and his brothers had all been killed by the Germans early in the war. Then it had been his turn to go into the army. He was still an adolescent when he left his village, and although he had since grown into a man and witnessed all kinds of horror, his longing for home had never diminished.

He showed us photographs he had carried with him during the battles of Stalingrad and Leningrad, when the Russians had at last succeeded in driving the Germans back. He described his village, the friends he had there, his favourite walks and pastimes when he was growing up. Any incident could precipitate the flow of his reminiscences. Perhaps this was something else he and my aunt shared. During the months of loneliness he had reworked his memories, expanded them, and kept guard over them. In normal times these would have been overlaid with newer experiences, but in the midst of war he preferred to hold on to them until they had flourished to such an extent that he could no longer contain them in his head.

His meeting with us provided the necessary outlet.

With great relief it all came spilling out. The age of his listener was not important. Many times when he and I were together, he would talk to me as he talked to my aunt or my mother, and I would feel flattered by this intimacy between us and hide the fact that I understood very little of what he said.

One day, as a special treat, my aunt prepared a favourite dish of Yuri's, made of mushrooms and cream. It reminded Yuri of the woods near his village, and the mushrooms that grew there in great abundance. My mother had also enjoyed picking mushrooms as a girl, and they began to compare their hunts and the special, memorable specimens they had discovered.

As they incited each other through a mutual pleasure in this subject, Yuri became more and more excited, as if he were actually about to discover a rare, hidden growth. My mother, on the other hand, was affected in a different way. She grew sadder and quieter, and soon Yuri was the only one left talking.

He noticed her changed mood and stopped, surprised.

"What is the matter," he asked her. "Have I said something to upset you?"

"No, no," she assured him. "It gives me great pleasure to listen to you, it's only that . . . . "

"Only what?" he persisted, and so, reluctantly, not wanting to ruin for him the pleasure of his reminiscence, she answered.

"Well, you see," she answered, "you will return to your woods one day. Mine will never grow again."

Yuri, who could not bear the thought that there were pains he could not alleviate, did not answer her, or so it seemed at the moment. He turned to me and picked me up. I saw that he had twisted his face into one of the funny masks that always delighted me. But this time I knew our game was different. We were not playing merely for our own pleasure. My mother was our audience and her laughter was to be our applause. I understood this as well as if he had whispered instructions in my ear, and I co-operated fully, going along with him in the pretence that the game only involved the two of us.

III

YURI WAS NOW part of our household. He still slept in the army barracks, but he was with us every day. At night, an extra plate of food waited for him. When he arrived at last, he would unbutton his tunic, pull off his boots, and sigh like a man who had come home. There was no electricity then, and we often sat in the dark, talking. I would fall asleep listening, and then Yuri would help my mother put me to bed. Sometimes he managed to get fuel for our lamp. Then Yuri and I would play while my aunt mended clothes and my mother worked on her translations.

After the first weeks in Dobryd, the Red Army established control over the town and its surrounding region, and there was little to keep the soldiers busy. Yuri, with time on his hands, would now be in and out of the house, like any member of the family. When he came, he was never idle. Often he would arrive early in the morning, just as my aunt set out for the marketplace, carrying bags of merchandise, odds and ends to sell, or to exchange for fuel or food. He would take the bags from her and carry them to the market.

There he would help her to set up the little kiosk and spread her wares.

Often they would meet soldiers along the way, friends of Yuri's who found his attachment to us slightly ridiculous. They teased him and laughed at him when they met him like this, carrying bags of cast-offs for an elderly lady, but Yuri remained perfectly at ease. He laughed at himself as easily as his friends did and went right on doing what had to be done without any sign of embarrassment.

Once, however, there was trouble. Yuri had just deposited my aunt, with her bags, in her usual place. Next to her, one of our neighbours sat in a make-shift shelter selling cigarettes. A Russian officer, one of Yuri's superiors, bargained with the woman about the price. She refused to lower it. The officer became angry, especially when he noticed that my aunt and Yuri were witnesses to his haggling. In disgust, he threw down the handful of cigarettes he had chosen. They spilled everywhere on the ground. The woman began to berate him as she bent to pick them up, quietly, however, since her fear of him restrained her anger. Even so, he heard her. He turned around and came back.

"How dare you insult a Russian officer? You're lucky I don't have you arrested for trying to rob our soldiers."

The woman muttered something, a plea perhaps, since she seemed ready to fall on her knees before him. Her submissiveness only incited him further. "That's enough. Stop whining. You don't fool me with your meekness. I know your kind. You were happy enough when we came and freed you from the Germans but already you're robbing us. All you Jews are the same. You live for money. It's no use expecting you to have honour or loyalty. You'd sell your own people if you had the chance."

The officer's voice had carried, and now there was quite a crowd around him and the unfortunate woman. Her cheeks were as flushed as his, but her eyes were downcast, her lips pressed together. Silence remained her only defence.

Yuri walked over to the officer and put his hand on the man's shoulder. "Excuse me, captain, but you have no right to say any of the things you've been saying. You should apologize to these women."

"Apologize? Why, you little worm, who the hell are you? What right do you have to correct my behaviour? Do you know what I can do to you for this? You've been hanging around with Jews so long you've forgotten how to behave with Russians."

"No comrade, I have not forgotten anything. It's you who need to be reminded of certain things. This lady"—Yuri pointed to my aunt—"has given her son to fight the Germans. All these people have lost relatives to our common enemy. They've suffered enough. It's not right to abuse them any more."

The captain was speechless for a moment. Then, suddenly aware of the crowd, which was growing larger than ever, he turned to Yuri and ordered him to follow. We all watched as they walked away briskly. Some of the children wanted to run after them, but they were quickly and decisively restrained. As soon as Yuri and the captain were out of sight, discussion broke out all around us. Some accused the woman of bringing on new troubles. Others vented their anger on the captain. My aunt was certain she would never see Yuri alive again.

In the evening, however, he showed up at our house at the usual time. He laughed and hugged my aunt as she poured out to him all the fearful situations her imagination had placed him in throughout this long day. Of course, he had been subjected to a severe tongue lashing; that was to be expected, but it really had not been very bad. The captain was hot-tempered and proud, but essentially a good man. In fact, Yuri warned my aunt, she should not be too surprised if the captain came to the market one day and apologized.

As it happened, the captain never came again to the marketplace, either to apologize or to shop. Yuri had over-estimated him. Like many of the younger soldiers, Yuri had great faith in his countrymen, in their goodness, their kindness, their great potential for perfecting the world they lived in. When my mother and my aunt explained to him how they saw the incident, as an outbreak of a disease that was at the best of times merely contained and not eradicated, Yuri would never agree with them. The captain, he insisted, was really a good fellow, if a little foolish. In no way did he speak for other Russians.

Their discussion about the captain went on for some days after the incident. It was dropped finally because they could not convince each other. But it returned in another form when we were preparing to leave Poland. Now, however, in the interest of preserving their friendship, the argument was pushed out of the way. The only reminder of the incident was the captain's aide. He shopped in the marketplace for his superior, but he always paid promptly, and without hesitation.

The next crisis went beyond mere insult. The captain may have disappeared from our lives, but Yuri's role as our protector continued. One night we were in the kitchen where we usually sat in the evenings.

My mother often worked there while we kept her company. She brought her work home with her, and in order to have some light to work by she received an extra supply of kerosene. The lamp was lit and her papers were spread before it. Nearby, my aunt sat sewing, while on the floor Yuri was teaching me how to play chess.

Suddenly my mother jumped from her chair and it toppled over to our chess board. I looked up and saw that the papers were on fire. My mother was hitting the flames with her hands, but to no effect. Yuri was at her side quickly. Before my aunt or I had recovered from the shock of the fire, he had put it out. But he was too late. The papers had been destroyed.

We were terrified. My mother's employer was a capricious and irritable man who inspired fear in everyone who worked for him—soldiers and civilians alike. He was quite capable of handing out the most extreme punishment, for an act as inconvenient to him as the one that had just occurred.

Again, Yuri was the first to recover. He walked over to my mother and took both her hands in his. "Don't be afraid. I'll go with you tomorrow and explain everything."

"You can't do that, Yuri," argued my mother. "You've already gotten into trouble because of us. I can't allow you to get involved any further. I was responsible for those papers and I must tell the colonel what happened."

"That's all right. You can do all the talking, but I'm coming along just in case. Your Russian is not all that good, you know. If you get excited or frightened, then the right words may not come. If I'm there, I can help you."

My mother smiled at Yuri and I felt the tension

lessen around me. It had become a frequent source of amusement among us that although my mother was not Russian, she often had to help Yuri with his reading. The war had cut off his education when he was still in his early teens, although, like most Russians, he retained a deep reverence for learning and books. When books from Moscow began to come through to the army base in our town, Yuri launched himself into a determined effort at self-education. Eager as he was, learning was hard work for him. His hands and his mind had grown used to other kinds of tasks, and he was very impatient with his own clumsiness. My mother helped him when she could, with encouragement and direction, and he often teased her about being a harsh teacher.

His reason for going along with her now was so inadequate that it expressed his good will better than anything. My mother gave way. The next day they set out together, my mother carrying the charred, blackened papers, while Yuri held the kerosene lamp.

The colonel, impassive, listened to their story and dismissed them without a word. Yuri and my mother did not know what to expect. Then, a week later, soldiers came to our flat and connected our electrical lines. That evening, while we were still marvelling at the change in our lives, the colonel himself arrived. He looked around, touched the new light and turned to leave. With the door open behind him he turned back again to look at my mother. "A translator for the Russian army cannot live like a peasant," he declared. Without waiting for a response he left. Ours became the first civilian dwelling in town to receive electricity.

IV

I BEGAN TO have nightmares about my mother. Night after night I saw her being captured by the military police and imprisoned. Whenever I had this dream, I would wake up shouting her name, but when she came into my room I couldn't bring myself to describe the images that frightened me.

I decided to tell Yuri about my fears. I was too young to realize that my confession might put him in an awkward situation. True enough, he loved us, but he was also an ardent Communist, devoted to the Red Army. Yet I was so sure of his attachment to us that it did not occur to me to wonder how he would react to the news that my mother was stealing from that army.

We often went for long walks together. On one such occasion, when we were alone far from other people, I spilled out Elsa's story, my mother's answer, and the fear with which I now lived. Yuri heard me out with a serious face. He did not try to make me laugh about my fears. Nor did he seem surprised by what I told him. Had he known all along about my mother's trips?

We had come to a stone seat in the walls of the old fortifications. Yuri sat down and took my hands in his. Our faces were level. "You did well to speak to me, but now you must promise never to mention this to anyone else." I promised quickly, impressed by his earnest expression and the sadness in his eyes.

"What your mother is doing is wrong, but these

are very special times. Today, right and wrong are not exactly what they are in times of peace. Your mother has to care for you and your aunt. Right now the army pays her very little—it doesn't have more—so she does what she can to keep you warm and fed. In this way she is doing the right thing. Someday the state will take care of all its people and no one will have to steal. The war is not over yet, but it will be soon. Then peace and prosperity will come to all of us."

Yuri's eyes were no longer sad. His face had changed into the familiar faraway expression that always accompanied his dreams about the future. It suddenly struck me that my aunt looked just like this when she talked of her summers as a young girl. The resemblance troubled me. What was the link between my aunt's lost past and the future Yuri promised me?

"Someday," he went on, "everyone will be free and happy." I wanted to believe him and soon all my doubts disappeared. My nightmares stopped. I waited, certain that Yuri would help us.

He did not fail me. Without telling us, he began to work at getting us out of Dobryd. It was, of course, the only solution. As long as my mother remained in Dobryd, there was no way he could make it unnecessary for her to travel. She had obtained her job only through Yuri's intercession. It paid very little, but there were others, as qualified as she, who would have replaced her eagerly. The war had forced everyone to steal and use the black market. There was no other way.

Somewhere else, however, where conditions were easier, we might have a chance for a more normal life. The town Yuri chose was in the newly acquired German territories. It was relatively undamaged, and it had seemed to Yuri that there were enough abandoned goods and property to assure our comfort.

He arranged to be transferred, and when he had actually received his orders he rushed to our house to tell us the good news. To his surprise, my mother and my aunt listened to him with apparent dismay. For a moment, even Yuri's enthusiasm seemed to falter.

There were hardly any valid reasons they could offer Yuri to explain their reluctance to leave Dobryd. Under its present annexation to Russia, the town had lost its national and linguistic ties to Poland. It had acquired a new Russian name, and they could no longer use their native language in the streets of the town where they were born. Each day they were forced to walk through the ruins of their own past. But none of this mattered. Their attachment to this piece of land was intense and animal-like. They could not bring themselves to leave.

V

THEN SOMETHING TERRIBLE happened.

My aunt's son, Alexander, had been handed over to the Germans by the Ukrainian partisans with whom he had joined forces. The Germans had executed him.

I was away when the letter arrived bringing this terrible news. I came home some time later and I heard my aunt's cries even before I reached our floor. As I approached our door the screams increased and I heard other voices moaning. Terrified, I rushed in and headed for the kitchen. I never reached it. A neighbour grabbed me up and carried me out of the apartment.

But I had already had a glimpse of my aunt transformed into a strange mad woman. Her hair, which she always kept neat and braided, even when she slept, hung loose and in disarray. Her clothing was torn, and blood trickled from her mouth; I was told later that in her first moments of grief she had knocked out one of her teeth. Hearing her screams, the neighbours had rushed in and held her arms to keep her from injuring herself further. For a long time she could not be left alone.

I stayed in a neighbour's apartment. Although everyone tried to hide my aunt's madness from me, I constructed my own picture from the gossip I overheard and from the screams that occasionally reached me. I was sad about my cousin's death, but the transformation in my aunt weighed on me much more heavily.

I had been separated from my cousin Alexander for several months. His physical presence had become distant and vague, so that his death seemed a mere continuation of our separation. In any case, I knew very little about death in general. I had always been kept away from it, deliberately, so that somehow I had lived through the war with less sophistication and morbidity than might have been expected.

My feelings about my aunt were another matter. The glimpse I had had of her as the neighbours restrained her terrified me. The notion of death seemed pale and harmless compared to my aunt's grief. Every day I asked to see her, but at the same time I felt relieved when my request was not granted. One evening my mother came for me and told me I could return to the flat. My aunt was better, she said, but she was not well. I would have to be very careful not to upset her. For a start, I must never mention Alexander's name, nor remind her of him in any way.

I saw my aunt that night and she looked calm, but very pale and thin. Still, she managed to smile at me. From then on I spent all my time with her. Everyone agreed that she revived only in my presence.

A strange pact was formed during the days I sat near my aunt's bed. My mother abdicated her control over me in favour of my aunt, as the price of my aunt's cure. My aunt, as she recovered, began to use her weakness as a form of blackmail whenever it seemed my mother was about to reclaim me. Years later my mother bitterly regretted this arrangement, but by then it was too late to alter it.

During my aunt's convalescence Yuri had finally persuaded my mother to leave Dobryd. My aunt agreed and we left as soon as she could walk.

On a cold, clear winter morning we boarded a train with hundreds of other Polish families. Most of them, because they had chosen to remain Polish citizens, were being moved by the Russians from eastern territories they had annexed to the new Polish territories seized from Germany. The train thus became a symbol of patriotism and loyalty to most of the people on it. The Russian troops who accompanied the train were jeered and insulted. They kept to themselves.

The trip took a long time. It seemed to me we were travelling to a very distant place. The train stopped and started constantly. We were crowded together in cars without seats. Noise and confusion characterized the entire journey. There were many children on the train. They ran about constantly and often became lost. Noisy arguments and fights occurred frequently as the trip went on and the people became familiar with one another.

Yet the general atmosphere seemed cheerful and ebullient. The news of an armistice had reached us on the train and it was greeted with tears and joy. There was much singing. Patriotic songs started out in one car and echoed down the line. Food and drink were passed around as in a family celebration. People on the train shared their supplies in a way that had become unknown during the war. The decision to share instead of to hoard demonstrated their belief in the future of Poland. A new life would begin for all of us in the captured German towns where we would live.

Our first sight of Bylau was encouraging. It was a real town, untouched by war. Buildings stood intact. Some of the houses had curtains on the windows. Occasionally these framed a bird cage or a plant. A light snow had fallen when our train pulled in, giving the town a special air of neatness and calm.

When we left the train, we saw that the town was almost deserted. Occasionally, we saw Russian soldiers marching, but no civilians. Most of the Germans had fled some weeks ago with their retreating armies, terrified by rumours that the Russians were avenging themselves on a helpless population. Those who had been unable to flee stayed out of sight. We were to be the town's new inhabitants.

We were given the key to the house that was to be our new home. It was small and neat, with a garden. The street was lined with trees. A stone church and a school house framed it at either end. The family who had lived in the house seemed to have left abruptly, as if they had gone away for a weekend and expected to be back shortly. All their belongings remained, and in the kitchen we found pots half-filled with food that had just begun to decay.

My first quick run through the house impressed me. In contrast to our flat in Dobryd, this house was full of luxuries. We found stacks of linen, dishes, pots, toys, books, furniture—all the essential props of everyday life. It seemed incredible to me that these were now ours. For a long time I expected the rightful owners to come forth momentarily and claim their belongings. But after a while, these objects became as ordinary to me as they must have seemed to their original owners. I felt we had reclaimed them for our own.

A few days later, Yuri joined us. He looked around our new home, marvelling at our changed surroundings, as pleased as a child with every new discovery. My mother and my aunt watched, amused, as he insisted on looking into every hidden corner and closet in our new home.

I was as enthusiastic as he was. I followed behind as he made his inspection, my own feelings reflected in his face. When he had seen enough, he picked me up and we went spinning around the room in our special private dance.

Then he called for a celebration. The table was set and decorated with our new acquisitions. Yuri had brought us a bottle of vodka and a long sausage. Everyone's glass was filled, even mine, and Yuri's first toast celebrated the end of the war. Quickly, however, he noticed that my aunt's eyes had filled with tears and he launched into a long story about some of his recent adventures.

As much as he tried to amuse my mother and my aunt, the party never became a very happy one for them. They, in turn, tried not to spoil his pleasure, but a mood of sadness gathered over our table. I was only dimly aware of what my mother and my aunt must have felt that night, celebrating the armistice in the midst of a strange German town. Yuri and I sensed the weight of their feeling crushing our joy. Somehow, I resented their past, which always intruded and spoiled the present. This feeling became even more intense in me in later years.

Later that night, when we had gone to bed, some of Yuri's friends came to the house and a real party began. There were many toasts; there was music, laughter and singing. I lay in bed in the room that was still strange to me, soothed and comforted by the sounds of the party. I fell asleep, suddenly, in the middle of a Russian song about Moscow, as I tried to memorize its lyrics.

VI

WE LIVED IN Bylau for four years. During that time I moved further and further away from the past and into the comfortable world of ordinary childhood.

Our household now included my father's brother Zygmund, who had returned from Russia at the end of the war to live with us. My mother's brother's daughter, Olga, came to Bylau to study medicine, and her weekends away from university were spent with us. We were now a real family. My mother had a well-paid job with the interim Russian government. My uncle managed a food co-operative. We lacked very little.

The greatest change came when I began to go to

school. My mother had sent me to a private school, run by nuns, since she had little respect for the state schools. They were at that time mainly indoctrination centres. The private school was for girls only, and we all dressed alike in sailor uniforms. Here I felt I had finally found a place where I could blend in and become an anonymous part of an identical, happy group.

Sometimes, when we were all working at the same task, I would see myself in the group and marvel at how well I was playing the role of a happy, conforming little schoolgirl. I felt almost smug about the way I had separated my inner, real life from this play-acting. Usually I sensed, however, that such distinctions were dangerous to my well-being and I willed them away, just as I did with night-time demons.

But my efforts were not always totally successful. Occasionally, in spite of my self-protective tactics, the past would burst into my life, a frightening intruder I was helpless to turn out.

One day when I was alone in the house after school, the doorbell rang. I opened it and found myself tightly embraced by a small peasant woman who was a stranger to me. She followed me inside, and when she realized I did not recognize her she began to hug me again. All the while she poured out a torrent of words I barely understood, but which I recognized to be Ukrainian.

My aunt found us like this when she came in a few minutes later. I saw her freeze as she caught sight of our guest. Before my aunt could move, the woman rushed over and fell to her knees before her. She pressed my aunt's hands to her lips, but my aunt's face remained unresponsive. The two women went into the kitchen and I was sent out of the house on an errand. I hurried back quickly, my curiosity about our strange visitor now fully aroused.

It was dark when I returned to the house. The woman was still there. My mother was home now as well. We ate together and I sensed that the adults refrained from talking in my presence. When I was quickly dispatched to bed after dinner, my suspicions were confirmed.

From my room, I could hear my mother and my aunt talking to the strange woman. Their voices were now very animated. My aunt's and my mother's voices sounded hard and cold, while their visitor seemed to be pleading with them. Then a woman's name caught my ear—Manya. There was something very familiar about it. I knew it, but how?

I heard my mother's voice rise in anger. "I owe you nothing. Do you think I've forgotten those last months in that awful barn? When my child was so weak she couldn't stand up, you demanded my wedding ring, the only thing I had left from my husband, before you would give her some milk. There was a time when she cried from hunger every night, and I promised myself I would kill you if I ever had the chance. Be thankful to leave here alive."

My mother's words, and the hatred in her voice frightened me. I heard the woman trying to answer her, but I was no longer listening. That child who had cried in hunger was me. And the strange woman who had once held the power of life and death over us was the same person who now sat in the kitchen weeping.

Manya! She had terrified me. I had seen her as a brutal force which left the adults around me helpless and cowering. Yet, much as I feared her, I awaited her arrival every night with impatience. If she was very late, the waiting became unbearable. Much as I feared her, I had learned very quickly that Manya also fed us. Without her visits there was no food. The nights she didn't come seemed worse than the occasional searches which threatened to reveal our hiding place.

Was she really here now, in our house? For a moment a wave of panic overwhelmed me and I shivered under the warm quilt. Then between my old memory of the cruel Manya and my present perception of her as small and humble, another image inserted itself—the portrait of Manya as a sad, ostracized girl, driven by visions of revenge. My aunt had drawn it for me during the months following our liberation and I had appropriated it with great interest for my own gallery of fantasy figures. In these stories she was somehow distinct from the Manya I had known, cleansed of the evil and terror I had associated with her in the past.

She had been born out of wedlock to a peasant woman in one of the villages that belonged to my grandfather. Illegitimacy was too common to be a stigma but Manya grew up an outcast for reasons other than the circumstances of her birth. Her mother was poor, awkward and dull, and she was treated with the cruelty that was usually accorded the feeble-minded in that region. Manya, although quick and bright, was treated in the same manner, simply for being her mother's child.

When she was fourteen years old she came to my grandfather and asked him to help her get away from the village. My grandfather found her a job as a servant in one of the large hotels in Carlsbad, a fashionable resort of the time. He bought her a one-way ticket, gave her some money, and put her on the train, certain that this was the last time he would ever see her.

Some ten years later, to everyone's surprise, Manya returned with a small child. Its father had been one of the hotel guests whose rooms Manya had cleaned, and whose boots she had polished. No one knew why Manya had chosen to return to a place where she had been so badly treated. From the start she kept very much to herself. The other peasants left her alone after a while, but whenever she appeared amongst them they laughed at her, for what they considered to be her false airs of superiority acquired in her years of service.

After her return she supported herself as a seamstress—a skill she had acquired as mysteriously as everything else. She was very good at it and she did not lack for customers. Her work brought her often to Dobryd, where she purchased her supplies and where most of her clients lived. My grandfather, after losing his estates when the Russians occupied Poland in the 1920's, now lived in Dobryd, and Manya often stopped at his house. She was always received with kindness, and there were usually gifts for her daughter and some sewing for her to do. Whenever there was a forthcoming marriage in the family, Manya would install herself in the house for several weeks to help with the preparations for the bride's trousseau. Here, as anywhere else, she would remain withdrawn, barely talking, and my grandparents knew as little about her as did her neighbours in the village.

In spite of her lack of contact with other people, she was extremely alert and observant. She read about the persecution of Jews in Germany and anticipated the same situation in Poland. As a result, she was one of the first to realize how desperate the plight of some of her best customers might soon become. In 1938, before the German invasion into Poland, she foresaw the danger that was about to threaten their lives. She understood how willingly and extravagantly they would soon pay for shelter of any kind.

At the time she confided her motives to no one. But months later, when her plan was in force and we were at her mercy in the loft, it became her special delight to talk to us about her dreams. Perhaps it was the sight of her captives in agony, for these people had once considered her far beneath them and now their very lives hinged on her whims. Part of her revenge was already realized. The rest would follow.

Her boasts were always received in silence. She didn't require any participation or encouragement for her pleasure. Our presence was enough. Nor did it matter how many times she told the story. She always relived it with great intensity. Her face would change from anger to hatred and finally to an expression of joy, as she foretold the triumphs that awaited her and her daughter after the war.

The hide-out was the beginning. It would lead to reprisals against a society that had always victimized her. By hiding rich Jews, she could earn huge sums of money. There was no reason why, by the time the war was over, she should not have sufficient funds to purchase the very hotel in Carlsbad where she had worked. This was the dream she had nurtured through all those silent hours. As owner of the hotel she would make up for all the misery she had known. Her own daughter would grow up to be as desirable a young lady as those whose white boots she herself had cleaned.

With the money, the hotel and her daughter's glorious future, she would have her revenge on everyone—on the stupid peasants who had mocked her since her birth, the guests of the hotel who saw her only as an object of servitude, the men who had abused her and her mother before her, and the rich in Dobryd whose houses she had to enter through the back door and whose cast-off clothes she had to accept gratefully.

Manya began to make her preparations. Her objective was to create a secret hiding place that would hold as many people as possible. The fact that she lived like a hermit on the fringes of the village, ostracized by the other villagers, became her main asset. At about this time the Germans proclaimed that anyone who gave shelter to Jews was subject to the death penalty. This had no effect on Manya's plans. She was living out her secret dream, happy as never before, and no threat could spoil it.

The place she chose for her shelter was a barn a few yards behind her house. The barn was unused, and screened by tall trees. After she had bought it for a small sum, she installed a cow in it, and a goat and some chickens, so that it would be no different from other barns in the region. At night she worked in the hayloft, extending the floor to create a false ceiling. The area between this ceiling and the roof was to be the shelter. She padded it entirely with straw for insulation and soundproofing. Next she began to lay in supplies, mainly sacks of potatoes and flour. When all was ready, she carefully drew up a list of those whom she considered likely to be most profitable as potential clients. Then she set about contacting them.

My grandfather was no longer a wealthy man, but he was approached by Manya in what was to be perhaps her sole gesture of sentiment. The evening she came to see him with her surprising offer she urged him not to hesitate. She already had enough willing and anxious lodgers to permit her to pick and choose. For the others, her selections were made on the basis of their gold supply and how much nourishment they would require. She was willing to make an exception for my grandfather, but he must be quick about it.

My grandfather, although touched by Manya's offer, did not accept it for himself. He had simply lost his desire to go on living in a world where everything seemed distasteful to him, and where most of the values he had always cherished were turned to mockery. In any case, he was seriously ill with diabetes, and since he felt that he was going to die soon anyway, he chose to spend his last days in his own home. My grandmother would not go anywhere without him. Of his family, the ones most in danger seemed to be my aunt and her son. Young men Alexander's age were then the main target of the sporadic raids the Germans made on the local population. It was decided that she, along with Alexander, would accompany Manya to the loft.

VII

WHEN MY AUNT left Dobryd with her son to hide, it was not expected that anyone else from the family would join her. However, conditions in Dobryd deteriorated quickly. It soon became necessary for my mother to seek refuge too.

My mother was now living with her parents. My father had left Dobryd to join the Russian army before the Germans had confined Jews to their ghetto. There was no one else to look after her parents, and so she found herself in the ghetto in charge of a household consisting of two elderly sick people and an infant.

There were still a few people outside the ghetto with whom she maintained contact. At night, risking death, she would make her way to an isolated point in the barbed wire fence to exchange a few words with someone from the outside world. In this way she learned what the Germans had in store for us in the next few days.

Their plan was to liquidate the entire Jewish community. In a day or so, when the necessary transport cars arrived, they would evacuate all those still able to work. They were to be sent to concentration camps. The others, the old, the sick and infants, were to be killed.

My mother realized that she had to make an attempt to escape from the ghetto before its destruction. She knew this meant she would have to abandon her parents; they were both resigned to dying and had no desire to save themselves. My grandmother prayed daily for death. There was very little hope, my mother knew, of getting out of the ghetto alive or of making her way to my aunt's hide-out. Still, she preferred this slim hope to sitting and waiting for the blow to fall.

She had little time to plan and no time to hesitate. All exits were being closed around her. The very next night, with me in her arms, and some small supplies, she made her escape. Fortunately, it was a dark night. She managed to cut through the barbed wire and get through to the other side without being seen by the guards. Once outside, she heard shots coming from inside the ghetto. For a moment she was terrified, convinced they were shooting at her. She hid in a doorway and as the shooting intensified, now accompanied by screams, she realized the destruction of the ghetto had begun.

She headed for a house nearby where one of her Christian friends awaited her with a change of clothing. Disguised as a peasant woman she began her journey towards Manya's shelter. Soon she found herself in the open countryside. For the next two weeks she continued to make her way to Manya's village, moving only at night, travelling in the shelter of wooded areas. She had grown up on this land and now she used her familiarity with it to help her survive. She found enclosures for us to sleep in, and herbs and leaves to nourish us.

Twice she was spotted and stopped. Once a German patrol intercepted us. She managed to get away by convincing them that she was indeed a peasant woman taking her child to a doctor. The second time a group of partisans stopped her. She could not fool them as she had the Germans, and this time she bought her freedom and even some food with the money she had taken from my grandfather's house.

At last she found herself outside Manya's village, and when it grew dark she made her way to the farmhouse.

The loft was by then well filled. The week before, however, someone had died of typhus. Manya could certainly have found a wealthier replacement than my mother. Also, she had previously excluded all children from her shelter. They were too troublesome, she felt, and they could not be relied upon to keep quiet during the searches by the German patrols. Nevertheless, there we were, the granddaughter and daughter of the one man to whom she felt any loyalty.

She knew it meant certain death for us if she refused us, so she relented and took us in.

Our acceptance in the shelter was still not assured. Its first occupants, like any early settlers, closed ranks amongst themselves and were scornful and hostile to those who came after. Most of all they were wary of accepting a child, who so obviously could endanger their lives.

While my mother and my aunt waited, and comforted each other, the argument about our fate raged around them. Luckily for us, the man who had become a kind of unofficial leader of the group was a close friend of my father's. The others finally gave way before his insistence. In a symbolic gesture of acceptance he led my mother and me up to the loft and pulled the ladder up behind us. A place was made for us among the twenty or so people who already lay there. We were given enough space in which to sit or stretch out. The slant of the roof was such that it did not permit any normal-sized adult to stand upright. We spent the next two and a half years there.

VIII

I REMEMBER THAT period with the vagueness of a half-forgotten dream, but I am convinced that I was often happy as a small child. When I try to picture what my life was like, I always see myself surrounded by people who gave me much attention and affection. Their presence protected me from the physical restrictions and hardships I experienced.

At first it was only my mother, my aunt and my

cousin Alexander who took turns amusing me. Then the others, a few at a time, became involved with my activities. They had, after all, little else with which to distract themselves from the constant hunger and boredom. I suppose they also felt that if I were kept happy and amused there would be less danger of my giving them away with my cries. I was the greatest threat in their midst, but ironically, I was their principal source of distraction and joy as well.

Few children have ever had so many adults at their disposal as I did during my years in the loft. Soon they began to differentiate themselves for me, according to some specific skill that each one of them practised with me. Hania sang well, and knew by heart the words of many songs and poems I never tired of hearing. Misha became my favourite storyteller. In his repertoire there was one story in particular that always fascinated me. This was the story of Baba Yaga, a form of the primeval bad spirit whom all children in Poland are taught to fear. I was sure Manya was an incarnation of that spirit. Baba Yaga was a very clever sorceress, but since in our stories she was always beaten eventually, I felt confident that one day we would be free of Manya.

The woman I called Granny had the idea and the patience to teach me how to knit. The wool came from an old stocking that was ripped and rewound, and the needles had been whittled out of twigs. I knitted and reknitted the same piece of wool in all sorts of different ways, each time imagining a different purpose that it was to serve.

My cousin Alexander taught me to read and write. A pencil and paper were provided for this from other people's possessions. Someone, Alexander I think, wrote out a primer for me between the lines of a used exercise book. No child ever had a more appreciative or encouraging audience than I, when I exhibited my new skills before my many teachers.

We had no news of the outside. Our only contact with the world beyond the loft was Manya, who came each night to bring us fresh water and bread. There were, of course, frequent patrols, coming so close sometimes that we were certain they could hear our heartbeats through the thin layer of straw that separated them from us. Once I remember bayonets being thrust up through the straw, but we were never discovered. The patrols, dangerous as they were, provided almost our sole excitement. After each search there would be a mood of rejoicing in the loft, and I would be praised and hugged for knowing so well how to keep quiet and still.

At night, those with any strength left went down from the hayloft into the barn for some exercise. Once, when I stood at the edge of the loft watching the others below, I experienced a dizzy spell and fell, breaking my arm. A splint was made for me and the bones grew together very quickly, but after this incident I was restricted even more in my movements since my mother feared another accident.

Another time I remember being ill with typhoid fever, a disease that plagued every member of our hide-out. Someone gave my mother two lumps of sugar for me, a treasure they had been hoarding against some extreme need of their own. My mother accepted the precious gift and cried.

After being cut off from the rest of the world for many months, the people in the shelter began to think less and less of the outside. At the beginning, there was much anxiety for relatives left behind, but slowly the hold of these ties loosened and an almost unreal spirit of happiness seemed to permeate our hiding place. A new kind of peace settled over everyone. There was little agitation or complaining. The adults spent their time sleeping, daydreaming, reliving the past, occasionally talking when their strength permitted. We lost all track of time; days disappeared into weeks, into months. Only the seasons, with their changes in climate, forced themselves into our consciousness.

Immobility and malnutrition had altered the people in the loft to something less than human, yet they scarcely seemed to notice or to regret their transformation. They had been forced to withdraw from the human race, slowly becoming more detached from it, until they felt only a vague nostalgia for their former lives. Death in these circumstances would have seemed very natural. External events, however, roused them eventually from this trance and reawakened the appetites of life.

No one told us the war was coming to an end. Manya would certainly not give us any information which might loosen her hold on us. Still, there were signs that could be read. The sounds of war were now within earshot, and this meant that the Russians were driving the Germans back to their own territories. The only firing we had heard until now had been that of the Germans executing the hostages in the village. Now the big Russian cannon were firing at the Germans. Every night we could hear their thunder as they shelled the German encampments. In the loft, each shell was greeted with elation. It didn't matter that one of these could have hit our barn as easily as the German fortifications. It was worth the risk to imagine our invincible tormentors fleeing from the barrage. Planes were soon heard as well, and then there was a daily exchange of bombing and the firing of anti-aircraft guns. We also heard the noise of the Germans retreating, and one terrible day we listened to the village people screaming with pain and terror as the Germans took their last revenge.

The lassitude of the past months gave way to a growing impatience. After all this time, would we live to see our liberators? One of the adults, the strongest in our group, began to venture out of the shelter at night to gauge the progress of the battle, but the people outside seemed to know as little as we did. They, too, were relying on the sounds of war for their information. One thing we did learn, however, was that gangs of Germans were roaming about dressed in Russian uniform pretending to be Russians. In this way they tricked some of the surviving Jews and partisans into betraying themselves. Soon the occasional sorties from the loft became more and more dangerous. The closer the end of the war seemed, the more vicious the Germans and their collaborators became.

As the possibility of freedom grew increasingly plausible, our situation in the loft was becoming ever more desperate. Manya had realized that her flow of gold would soon be cut off. The inevitable end of her rule over us drove her greed beyond its former limits. She was determined to extract every trace of wealth before she lost us forever. She announced to us that her food supplies had run out. After the daily plunder of the retreating Germans, the peasants had nothing left to sell. From now on, we must expect to pay dearly for every bit of food, and the rate increased with the approach of the Russian army.

No one dared venture out to look for food. Soon there were those in the shelter who no longer had money to give. Manya told them to leave, but she could not really drive them out. She lacked the physical force to remove them herself, and she could not betray them without also betraying those who still had some money left and putting herself in jeopardy for sheltering Jews. She decided to starve them out. Those who still had some means had to balance out the hunger of their companions with their own quickly diminishing funds.

The promise of freedom had resurrected the people in the loft. Everyone now wanted to live. They felt a hunger for life that they would never experience again with such intensity. The mood of peace and contentment was lost in this new frenzy.

Who can say what acts we might have witnessed in our shelter had this situation lasted longer than it did? As it was, these last weeks managed to erase most of the feelings of kinship and camaraderie that had developed among the inhabitants of the loft. In later years, these people who had once formed an entire universe amongst themselves avoided all contact with one another. None of them wanted to be reminded how far they had been driven by the extremity of their situation from the level of civilized human beings. They had no desire to remember how eager they had been to sacrifice one another to save their own lives.

Manya's desperation matched that of her victims. Relentlessly she hunted down every piece of gold in the shelter. When people pleaded that they had nothing left to give, she reminded them of the wedding band they were wearing or the earrings placed in their ears at birth, or any other valuable memento which had not escaped her eye.

At the end, when nothing remained, she abandoned us to our fate. We were left with no news, no food or water, while outside the fierce fighting continued day and night.

When Yuri and his battalion reached Manya's farm, they found her crazed with fear, barricaded with her daughter. The Germans, in their retreat, had raped the two of them. They feared the same treatment from the new invaders. Yet Manya was still sufficiently alert to suspect that the act of hiding Jews from the Germans might win her some favour with the Russians. She confided her secret to them. Our ordeal was over.

Although that day when my life really began, at the age of five, and the day of Manya's visit to Bylau were only three years apart, they seemed to me to have happened in different worlds, to different people. It was only by deliberately separating my present life from the first one that I could even bear to think of these events. It was also a way of trying to understand Manya's transformation and my own since our days in the loft. It seemed necessary for me to pretend I had nothing to do with that other child, or the other Manya. The world of terror and cruelty that had brought them together had never happened. The fact that I could listen to stories about the times in the loft, and even enjoy them, proved to me they had nothing to do with me.

I had expected to find Manya gone the next morning but she was still there. In the end my mother relented. Manya's misfortunes had softened her anger.

Manya's money was all gone. Her property had been taken over by the Russians, and the village turned into a collective. She worked from morning till night, and her daughter shared the same life. Carlsbad was now a government-run resort. Its clientele consisted of workers who had surpassed their production quotas.

My mother sent her back to the village the next day. Thereafter, she began to write us letters full of bitterness and complaints. They followed us to Canada when we moved there. Eventually they stopped, and in time, her daughter informed us of her death.

PART FIVE

I

WE LIVED IN Bylau for four years. Like most children when they are happy in a particular place, I had expected to live there forever. It seemed to me we had at last found a home where we belonged. Dobryd became more and more removed, and its presence in our lives appeared less important. Still, it was sufficiently close to us in time and in space so that it had not yet been surrounded by an aura of nostalgic seductiveness.

Most people in Bylau were, like us, immigrants from other parts of Poland. We were all building new lives, starting on the same basis. Old distinctions and divisions seemed not to count.

Perhaps because of its recent past, Bylau was a fiercely patriotic town. Traces of its German origins were being replaced by the symbols of Polish nationalism. The new inhabitants were all very patriotic. In government schools the children were drilled in national pride, and even in private schools we were taught to regard all other Slavic nations with disdain. It seemed inconceivable to me that we would ever leave.

Our family was much like the others. Externally,

at least, we had adapted and become involved in our new community. In actual fact, our place in that society was doubtful. The older I became, the more I was aware that the adults around me lived with a sense of foreboding. They regarded their surroundings with the uneasiness of people who live at the foot of a volcano. There had been slight rumblings in the last four years, but these were on a small scale and they could be explained in such a way as to make them seem harmless. It required a common crisis, shared by all the Jews in the town, to crystallize an awareness of how precarious our position in that society was.

One morning we noticed that our house had been marked during the night by a large red cross over the entrance. Soon afterwards we noticed this same cross in varying sizes painted outside other houses. What was ominous about it was that only the homes of Jews had been singled out in this way. Various interpretations of this fact were not long in coming, and the hearts of the survivors were once again gripped by terror.

They remembered, without anyone's mentioning it, that during the war it had been common practice for the Germans to mark certain houses with crosses. They would do this the night before a new transport was to leave for the concentration camps, and in this way the removal of those selected was facilitated.

New crosses were discovered all that day. With each one the evidence seemed more threatening. Meeting one another, each person confirmed what the other feared: the Poles were about to practise their traditional rite, the terrorizing and murder of Jews. Jews sought each other out, hoping that one of them would know more than the others, but they found no reassurances. The eyes of all the survivors mirrored the same image of dread. Everything they imagined was only too likely to happen.

In our house the mystery of the red crosses also evoked fear and dread. My mother and my uncle stayed away from work; if anything was to happen, we would at least be together. In the evening when Yuri arrived, he found the house dark and his friends filled with foreboding. For a moment he stood astonished, unable to understand the difference he saw in us. Then his expression changed to one of fear. Something dreadful must have occurred. "What is it? What happened? Is anyone ill?" he asked.

My mother told him the story of the crosses and described her fears. To our amazement, after he heard her out, he smiled in a way that seemed totally incongruous. He was too kind to tease us about our misunderstanding as he quickly explained it. The red crosses that had terrified us were nothing more than a way of distributing food parcels to war victims. The shipment which had just arrived was from an American Jewish relief agency. It was reserved for Jewish survivors. Since there were still no numbers on the houses, red crosses were painted to help identify the recipients.

That evening we laughed with Yuri, at ourselves, euphoric with the relief of people reprieved from reliving their worst nightmare. The effect of that incident however, was more profound than any of us suspected.

For a while it seemed the incident of the crosses was forgotten, but slowly it insinuated itself back in our lives. I began to hear my family talk of leaving Bylau, and my sense of belonging was shaken. My mother and my aunt returned to the subject daily, arguing with each other, trying to convince themselves. It was becoming impossible for them to stay in Poland, but it was equally difficult to leave.

If it was harder for them to leave than for other Jews, it was because of the way they had been brought up. Their father had seen to it that all his children knew their native land well and felt at home in it. He had travelled widely in Austria, Germany and England and he had observed that in those countries the Jews were well treated and respected. He was impressed by how well they were integrated into the ways and habits of their Christian neighbours. The Jews in Poland, he felt, were much to blame for their less enviable position. If after centuries of living side by side they continued to be hated by their Polish neighbours, it was because they persisted in leading their lives without any recognition of the language, customs and culture of the country which had been their home for hundreds of years. *300 years*

His cousins in Hamburg or Vienna had not ceased to consider themselves as Jews. Nevertheless, when they walked the streets of their towns, they looked and acted like other passers-by. They lived in integrated communities, they were educated in subjects other than the sacred texts, and they did not restrict their friendship to Jews. It was this kind of life that my grandfather wanted for his children.

He realized that his actions would scandalize most of the Jewish community and that he had no hope of convincing his wife. The marriage had been arranged by their parents when they were very young. He had first seen her at the betrothal ceremony. She had been very beautiful, the daughter of a rich and noble rabbinical family who counted amongst their ancestors great Talmudic scholars and a miracle rabbi. But after the first enchantment of living with her had worn off, he found her ignorant, superstitious and full of prejudices. She, for her part, suffered all her life from the fear that she had been married to a heretic who would drag her down with him to eternal condemnation. My grandfather concentrated all his hopes on his four children.

It was my grandfather's work that had first taken him out of the ghetto. He had started in the grain trade, buying from Polish landowners and selling to the rest of Europe. By the time his first child, my uncle Samuel, was born, he himself had become a landowner. From then on, he chose to live in the country. One of his partners took over the grain trade, and he occupied himself with every detail of running a large country estate which included several villages of peasants. My aunt remembered that as a small child she would ride with him in the morning, and every person they met would greet him with the greatest reverence. As a little girl, she was certain he was a king.

It was unusual for Jews to own large estates in Poland. For a great many years the laws had restricted this privilege to the Catholic aristocracy. My grandfather's estate had belonged for centuries to a family of Polish counts. They, like many Polish aristocrats, considered their own country a primitive, boorish place from which they wished to dissociate themselves. Some went so far as to refuse to teach their children their native language, considering it no better than a peasant dialect. French was the language of civilized people. They were hopeless Francophiles, and exile, to them, meant an enforced stay in Poland. The only binding tie they maintained with their country was the revenue they extracted from it, often in such a careless manner that in the end their mortgaged and neglected estates ceased to yield anything.

The Count H., who owned the estate my grandfather acquired, spent most of his time in Monte Carlo and Deauville. Through extravagant living and gambling he had ruined his inheritance. The idea of returning to Poland and working to improve the damage he had brought about bored him. The only acceptable solution that he saw was to sell the estate. The Count and my grandfather met in Warsaw, in what was to be the Count's last visit to Poland. The Count promised to arrange all the legal matters and my grandfather agreed to pay him an allowance for the rest of his life. The villages continued to bear his name, in suffix or prefix, while he enjoyed the more temperate climate of southern France.

In this country setting, distant from the claustrophobic atmosphere of the small-town ghetto, my grandfather was able to live as he pleased. Above all, he sought to give his children the best preparation for their life as Polish citizens. The children spoke Polish as their first language. They were sent to Polish schools and encouraged to bring home their classmates. Yet at home they were taught to have pride in their ancestry.

The children seemed to thrive in this atmosphere. They grew up confident and at ease with their environment. The boy, more than the others, seemed to have taken his patriotism to an extreme. When he graduated from secondary school he refused to continue his studies, since it would have meant going away to Switzerland for several years. He showed no real interest in anything except farming. As a child, he had often bribed the peasants who drove him to school to turn their carriages around and drive him back home with them. There he would follow them around all day, learning how to plough and helping them with the chores.

My mother and my aunt shared their brother's attachment to the land. This set them apart from other members of the Jewish community in Dobryd. They had some friends within this group, but more of their friends were Christian Poles. In fact, the family belonged neither to the Jewish nor the Christian community and these two groups regarded the family with some suspicion because of their unconventional ways.

The feeling of isolation and separateness which marked their upbringing was not the goal their father had sought for them. Yet they did not mind their singular position. In fact, it became a source of family pride. Years later, when my mother spoke of her family, she always concluded, "Your grandfather was a man ahead of his time."

The war had introduced them to another set of experiences which mocked my grandfather's ideals and the family's patriotism. They had loved the land, but the land had betrayed them. The neighbours and friends in whose trust they had placed their safety remained, at best, indifferent. Some had even collaborated with the invaders in hunting them down. In the end it was these memories, evoked by fresh incidents such as that of the crosses, which finally made them decide to leave Poland.

II

AFTER MANY YEARS away from Poland, my mother, like so many exiles, became a victim of nostalgia. The greater the distance between her and her home, the more she thought of it as the lost land of her youth, where she had been happy as she never would be again.

Polish culture became the standard by which she judged all others. She rarely missed any film or theatre company that came from Poland to Canada. She continued to read and reread the classic literature of Poland, especially its poetry, much of which she could recite by heart.

Side by side with this past, which she loved, the horrors of the war continued to haunt her. She relived these memories at night in terrifying, recurring nightmares. I heard the sounds of the nightmares before I knew what they meant, and they frightened me more than any of my private monsters. That low persistent moaning, the occasional screams of fear—what had they to do with my mother as I knew her? Later, when I understood what her nightmares were about and I learned what brought them on, I could still not reconcile the confident person she was in the daytime, with the sounds that came out of her bedroom at night.

I never really understood how all the love and hate she felt for Poland could continue to co-exist within her. She loved the language and hated those who spoke it. She refused any contact with the large Polish community in Montreal. She would never speak to any Pole who had been more than a child at the time of the war. This was to avoid the possibility, she explained, of talking to someone who had contributed to the betrayal of anyone she had loved. Her dislike of adult Germans never reached the proportions of her hatred of Poles her own age. These were her people, a generation she had once belonged to. She would never forget what they had done to her.

There were certain incidents she recalled more than others. Her mind returned to them again and again, as if her existence defined itself through the pain of those memories, and she reassured herself by probing to see if it was still there. When I was growing up and listening to her, it seemed to me often that in the background of my life there was a constant chorus of mourners. The steady and monotonous dirge of their lament gave me no peace. Perhaps it was intended that I should pick up and carry on the complaint of the betrayed. But at a certain age I saw myself as an offering on a memorial of hate, and I refused to have anything to do with it. I did not know then how powerful my mother's words had been, nor how deeply these stories of what had happened to the members of our family had penetrated my mind.

When the war broke out, my uncle Samuel, my mother's only brother, was living the kind of life he had always wanted to live, as a prosperous landowner, on good terms with his neighbours and his friends. He was certain they would protect him when the Germans came in search of Jews. In appearance, and in every other way, he resembled the Christian landowners of the district. There was no way the Germans could single him out.

In the winter of 1939 the German army reached the region where my uncle and his family lived. This was the beginning of the German occupation. They had not yet consolidated their hold on the countryside; the efficient grouping of victims for the purposes of destruction had not yet been set up. As they marched deeper into the country, their selection of victims was haphazard, and they were forced to rely to a great extent on the co-operation of the local population in rooting out "undesirables".

When they reached my uncle's village, they camped overnight in the mayor's office. The next morning a small patrol left the mayor's building and headed for my uncle's farm. There was a local guide with them, and they seemed to be informed of every detail that would facilitate their work.

The first thing they did when they arrived at the farm was to kill the dogs. My uncle and his wife, still lingering over their breakfast, were taken entirely by surprise. But their destruction was not as simple as the soldiers had anticipated. Samuel and his wife struggled fiercely. They called to their servants, but no one appeared. They continued to resist alone as long as they could. The Germans had intended to hang them in public. This was the custom at the outset of the war, in dealing with important local personages. But because of the fierce struggle they encountered, they were obliged to shoot their victims first. Only then were they able to carry out their plan.

They were hung in the town square, but because of the resistance they had shown, the Germans hung them by their feet and forbade anyone to cut them down for a week. They remained like this for the prescribed period, and the peasants, after they had gotten used to the horror of this sight, came regularly in the evening to gaze at them and to gossip near their swaying shadows. Small children ran beneath them and used them as targets for their stone-throwing. Eventually they were cut down and buried in an unmarked grave.

Their only daughter, Olga, was away at school, and managed to survive the rest of the war. After the war, when she and my mother first heard the story of her parents' death, they decided to hunt down those responsible for it. They set out together for my uncle's farm. When the peasants learned that my mother and my cousin were willing to pay for information, the response was overwhelming. All sorts of names were proposed to them as the possible informers. My mother and my cousin realized despairingly that because of the peasants' cupidity they would never be certain who had committed the betrayal. Thus, the attempt at revenge ended in frustration, and they left the village without even finding the place of burial.

My mother was also haunted by the death of cousin Alexander. The partisan group he had joined included several Ukrainians who were more notorious than the Poles for their hatred of Jews. They must have been hostile to him from the start because he was a Jew; however, they managed to conceal their hatred until it would be useful to them.

Then a member of the group was captured by the Germans and destined to be shipped off for hard labour. His comrades arranged his release by handing over my cousin in his place. One night they sent him out on a small sabotage mission in the railroad yard. The Germans were alerted. Alexander was caught and executed. One month later the war was over.

After the incident of the crosses, the voices of the betrayed began to haunt my mother more than ever.

She felt they were urging her to leave the land where she had suffered. In the end she accepted their counsel.

III

THE HARDEST PART about leaving was our separation from Yuri, a separation that in all probability would be final.

Soon after our arrival in Bylau, Yuri had gone back to his village. When he returned, after an absence of a few weeks, he was so changed no one dared ask him what had happened. Eventually he was able to tell us that his village had fallen victim to a German reprisal attack. The Germans had burned the village to the ground. The few young people who remained were sent to labour camps; the old were made to dig their own mass grave, and fell into it as they were shot.

My mother and my aunt knew what Yuri was feeling. They waited, and helped him through the familiar cycle of numbness, self-pity, rage and hatred. In the end, when he was consoled as much as he would ever be, they were his family and he was theirs.

Now they were talking of emigrating and leaving him behind. The closer they came to a decision, the harder it was for them to tell him. But at last he had to be told. His reaction was one of total incomprehension. It seemed incredible to him that a misunderstanding as trivial as the one of the crosses could lead us to such a decision. For him the war was over, the enemy vanquished. Now was the time to rebuild, to forget the past, to live with confidence in the future. They were mad to run away now.

"What will you do alone in a strange land?" he asked in bewilderment. "How will you live? Why leave now when your country is free?"

Night after night I heard them talking, my mother explaining what it meant to be a Jew in Poland: the betrayals, the fear, the enemy within that would never be driven out. History was clear-cut; its patterns seemed inevitable, yet each generation of Jews in Poland had to learn it anew. She had only just understood that. She couldn't remain, knowing that I would probably have to live through the same disillusionment and betrayals she had experienced.

Yuri had only one answer; what she said was true about the past, but things were different now. Everyone had changed, just as she had. It would be entirely different for me. If we stayed, I would belong here as much as anyone else. Did she really think I would feel more at home in some strange land where we knew no one, and whose language I couldn't even speak? No, it was precisely because of me that she must stay. For the children of communism, the future would be glorious. *70 years of communism in Russia*

I listened as they argued about my future and my heart was with Yuri. I loved him, I was happy with our life in Bylau, I liked my school, my friends. I didn't want to leave.

But my mother's voice told me there was little hope. Her bitterness was so overwhelming that often I did not even hear her words. It brushed aside Yuri's reassurances, his optimism, his political faith. The weight of my mother's experience was such that his words never touched its core. The more I listened to them, the more hopeless I felt. I knew nothing

Yuri said could stand up against the hatred that possessed my mother. The betrayals she had experienced cut so deep that only total separation could ease the wound.

My own feelings about Poland made the matter worse. My very reluctance to leave was reason enough for my mother to precipitate our departure. She saw my attachment as a trap. It prevented me from seeing my exclusion. I was blind, as she had been, and equally vulnerable to the blows the future had in store for me. The only way she could protect me was to take me away.

My mother's will overrode everyone's objections. In the end my aunt and my uncle agreed with her. My cousin, however, had just graduated from medical school and could not be convinced to accompany us. She was to make the journey ten years later, for the very reasons my mother had anticipated.

It was decided that we would move to Warsaw, where it would be easier for us to wage the long battle for an exit visa.

Yuri saw us off. He helped us onto the train and loaded our belongings into our compartment. Then came those last few moments when there is nothing left to do except say good-bye to someone you love and will probably never see again. That too, passed. The train pulled away. I leaned out, waving madly at a figure that reflected my motions back to me. Under the lights of the station, his hair and his military decorations gleamed as brilliantly as they had when I first saw him.

PART SIX

I

WE CAME TO a section of Warsaw near the foreign embassies. My mother felt this would give us a better chance of obtaining an exit visa. We didn't expect to be in Warsaw for any great length of time, and so we moved into a hotel. As it turned out, we remained there for a whole year.

The Hotel Bristol in 1949 was a world in itself. Outside, the city of Warsaw seemed vague and menacing. I was constantly warned not to venture from the hotel alone. From the window of my room I could see streets still in ruins, like those we had left behind in Dobryd. Here there was, in addition, the danger of unexploded bombs. The newspapers carried frequent stories and warnings about the threats to safety still lurking in the city.

At first I was made to go along with my family to the various waiting rooms where they spent their days. I found the confinement and boredom of these rooms sheer torture, and ended up making such a nuisance of myself that they agreed to leave me behind in the care of one of the hotel chambermaids.

My mother, my aunt and my uncle went off each morning as if to work, carrying envelopes stuffed with

documents and testimonials contrived to prove our
desirability as immigrants. Each would head for a different embassy to spend the rest of the day waiting,
often not daring to leave to eat for fear of missing
a turn.

In the waiting rooms and in the hotel rooms the
conversation of the hopeful emigrants always returned to the same theme—how to obtain proper
documents. Most people were in the same position.
All their legal records had been lost or destroyed during the war. Yet without these documents, life in the
post-war world was impossible. One couldn't do anything or go anywhere without them. Each day government officials insisted on demanding papers they
knew no longer existed, and so the only recourse was
to turn to forgers and false witnesses. It was an endless
process. In our family, for example, we were asked
almost every day to produce yet another kind of
record without which, it was explained, our case could
not be considered. In the evening, someone would
be found who, at a price, would supply us with the
papers we needed. Forging papers was certainly the
most flourishing industry of the time in Warsaw.

My family spent their days in the waiting rooms
of embassies, and in the evenings, like so many others,
they sought out the intricate paths of the shadow
bureaucracy. Every government official had his illicit
counterpart somewhere in Warsaw—a person who
earned his living by fulfilling the demands that the
government official set. Everyone involved—the official, the forger, the emigrant—played his part, aware
of one another's existence, yet publicly maintaining
the charade that this symbiotic network did not exist.

The emigrants themselves, trapped in the web of
the parasites who lived off them, developed their own

information network. The veterans of the waiting rooms instructed the newly-arrived on the particular whims or preferences of each official, and on how these were best dealt with. They knew where to obtain a birth certificate, or a letter from a non-existent brother, living in the country of one's choice, who would guarantee one's maintenance there. They were acquainted with people who specialized in being witnesses and who were equipped for this work by a talent for disguise and an ability to testify with persuasive sincerity to whatever was required.

Yet the waiting period was not all bleak for the people involved. Almost everyone we met shared a similar mood of elation. We were intoxicated with the promise of our future. The Hotel Bristol had a constant air of excitement and festivity about it. The public rooms were crowded late into the night. Conversations, discussions and arguments went on all around us, and strangely enough, I discovered they were not based on the past. For most of its inhabitants the hotel was a way station, and their attention was focused on the journey that was about to resume.

The noises and activity of the hotel seemed to me wonderfully exciting. I was soon free to explore it as I wished. Since we might be called upon to leave any day, there seemed to be no point in making long-term arrangements for me. I no longer went to school. Instead, my family and other people took turns giving me some sort of instruction.

My mother took it upon herself to teach me English, a language she had studied in school and perfected through travel. The only English book she could find was a copy of Oscar Wilde's *Lady Windermere's Fan*, probably left behind by some pre-war visitor. It became the text for our study of the English language.

Unfortunately, the world inhabited by Lord and Lady Windermere, the things they talked about and the idiom they preferred, had very little attraction for me at this age. I sat bored and restless as my mother read passages from the play, translated them for me, and then tried to have me repeat simple phrases. The lessons were mostly wasted on me, and their only noticeable result was a growing dislike on my part for the sound of this odd language my mother insisted I learn. It sounded ludicrous, compared with the "normal" sounds of the languages I already spoke. In spite of my mother's warnings, it seemed inconceivable to me that I would soon live in a place where no one spoke any Polish or Russian.

My uncle Zygmund, it was decided, was to teach me arithmetic. He had an unusual ability to retain in his mind long series of numbers and to perform with them, mentally, complicated calculations. In order to develop my capacities along similar lines, he insisted we must not use paper or pencil in our lessons. All the figures we worked with had to be memorized. In this way he hoped both to teach me arithmetic and to improve my memory.

When our lesson began he would give me several digits to add, subtract or whatever. If, as often happened, I became discouraged with my inability to remember the numbers, my uncle would try to revive my interest in the lesson by giving me a demonstration of the dazzling feats his own memory could perform. In a matter of seconds he would produce an answer to lengthy and complicated arithmetic problems, whose manoeuvres he would work out aloud for my benefit.

Another of his favourite methods was to use playing cards. His attachment to cards, I learned, was a holdover from the past, one of the few reminders left of his previous life. Before the war he had been something of a disgrace to his family. While his younger brothers studied or worked, he preferred to spend his time in the various fashionable spas of Eastern and Central Europe. His visits abroad had started on the pretext of ill health, which his mother ascribed to him as a result of a premature birth and a delicate childhood. Soon, however, he was indulging his taste for hotels and resorts beyond the demands of health, and even his mother could no longer justify them. Finally, his father, in order to give his son's activities some semblance of respectability, let it be known that he was profiting from his travels by furthering the family's business interests. The skills he acquired in his travels, a knowledge of the latest dances and a talent for cards, were not appreciated by his family, and as a result he spent less and less time at home.

The war had put an end to all that forever. He had survived by making his way to Russia. There he had been forced to join the army. For most of the war he was stationed in the Ural Mountains, where he was in charge of a supply depot. When the war ended, he had made his way back to Dobryd, only to discover that he was the sole survivor of his family. He had adapted to his new life with a facility that amazed all those who knew him before the war.

Somewhere in the hotel he had found a deck of cards. He could not resist incorporating them into our lessons. Whatever his original purpose in using them had been, it was forgotten. With great patience he taught me to play all the games to which he had been addicted in his youth, the games which had brought about constant friction with his parents. Once I learned to play them I enjoyed cards almost as much as he did. At times, when other men joined my uncle in playing, I was allowed to remain with them and watch. I felt very honoured.

I was also given piano lessons by a woman who, like us, was waiting for a visa. The only piano in the hotel was in the bar, and it was there that the lessons took place, usually in the morning when the room was closed to guests. The lessons themselves I found dull and endless, since they consisted of practising the same scales over and over. Nevertheless, I didn't mind. The room in which they took place compensated for the tedium of the lessons themselves.

While my fingers stumbled over the black and white keys, my eyes lingered with pleasure on the display of colour and form just beyond the piano. The arrangement of bottles in the hotel bar seemed to me one of the most beautiful sights I had ever seen. Whenever I could get close enough, I was content to gaze for a long time at the labels. Their rich colour and their names spoke to me of exotic places and strange adventures. The image of beauty conveyed to me by the sight of the bar was far greater than that promised by the instrument over which I laboured.

The bar room also intrigued me because of the sounds that came from it when it was occupied by its regular clientele. At the time we were there, the bar of the Hotel Bristol was the centre of Warsaw's social life. People gathered there for all sorts of reasons. Anyone passing through the town sooner or later made his way to the Bristol bar. It was always crowded and noisy.

The sounds of the bar diffused throughout the hotel from the afternoon until late into the night. During our entire stay in the hotel I never tired of listening to these sounds. The laughter and excitement they conveyed were intoxicating to me. Occasionally there was music. One song, an American one introduced to us by a u.s. soldier, became very popular. Someone played it every night. The song was "Give Me Five Minutes More", and I learned its lyrics without understanding what the words meant.

The song, and the noise and laughter that formed its background, excited my imagination. Just as someone might decide to learn a language simply because she liked its rhythm and cadence, I studied the sounds of adult pastimes reaching me from the bar. At night I lay in my room and listened to them as they filtered towards me, and it seemed that they held the promise of a new world, one to which I would soon go. The life I was about to leave behind was already becoming less and less real.

II

THE FREEDOM OF being alone in a large hotel delighted me. I never yearned to go outside. The interior of the building presented me with endless possibilities. In the beginning I wandered about by myself, trying to keep out of other people's way. Occasionally I would catch a glimpse through a half-open door of the rooms beyond and the people inside them.

These fragmentary visions of other people's lives and the settings in which they lived them fascinated me. Had I been bolder or more resourceful I would have been happy to spend all my time watching other people, even if they were only doing the same things

I saw in my own family every day. As it was, I had to be content with partially observed sequences, and the missing parts intrigued my imagination to the point where I often simply made them up. When my family returned in the evening, I would recount what I had seen, and my stories after a while grew so improbable that even when I told the truth it was impossible for anyone to believe me.

Very early in my wanderings around the hotel I came across other children. I got to know the ones who, like myself, were there more or less permanently, and we became friends. My new friends were a mixed group: children of the hotel staff, children of embassy officials and the children of guests. Housing in Warsaw was so scarce that the hotel was, in fact, an apartment house of one-room dwellings, with a communal dining room.

The children of the hotel used its corridors as other children use the city's sidewalks. The private rooms were too crowded for active play, and the public rooms were reserved for adults, so we were forced to take our games into the corridors. Language wasn't a problem. Some of the children went to school and others didn't, yet when we played together there were few allusions to the outside world. To my great delight, I discovered that my friends were as fond of roaming and observing as I was. Most of them, in fact, were more skilful at this pastime than I and they initiated me into their favourite look-outs. We were all incorrigible voyeurs, yet at the same time we were such innocents we hardly knew what to make of all we saw.

Soon, we developed our own sequence of events for the day. The mornings, for example, were best for visiting other rooms. At that time the chambermaids were busy making beds, and sweeping, and many of the doors remained open. Getting into these rooms, but keeping out of the chambermaids' way, became our special version of hide and seek. We had learned very quickly that certain hidden corners were never touched. There we would hide, breathing in dust, discovering bits of belongings from former guests, suppressing our laughter as the maids, unaware of being observed, behaved with a total lack of self-consciousness. It didn't matter what these women did, most of their gestures were exactly the same as those we saw in other adults. We stalked them with the same fascination that I once recognized in the faces of some other children observing a family of chimpanzees who ignored their presence.

In the afternoons we spied on some of the guests. We had our favourites amongst them and we made our rounds of their rooms with the same devotion that I felt a few years later for my favourite television heroes. Yet, as it sometimes happened, if they spoke to us in passing, we became uncomfortable and rushed to escape. In some ways we knew our idols very well —few of their belongs had escaped our examination—still, somehow it was essential to our game that they keep both their distance and their mystery.

Most of us were a serious blend of cynicism and ignorance. Because of the conditions of our lives we knew all about bribery, forgery and the constant necessity to dissimulate and lie. Yet we were strangely innocent when it came to sexual matters. I remember once telling my new friends how babies were made and born. I had learned this from my cousin as I was leafing through her medical texts. My friends, many of them older than I, listened to my explanation with expressions that told me they were hearing it for the first time. After that I was often asked to repeat my fabulous tale. Apart from the most elementary facts, we knew very little, and much of what we saw remained incomprehensible to us.

Just when I had totally accepted the life we led in Warsaw, my mother announced to me that our visas had been granted and that we would soon leave. The news completely upset me. Perhaps it was the idea of new farewells coming so close after the painful one with Yuri. Perhaps it was fear of where we were going. I was miserable and no one could comfort me. As the time of our departure drew closer, my unhappiness increased. The year in the hotel had seemed to me the happiest of my life. I couldn't bear the thought of leaving my friends, never to see them again.

On our last day in the hotel my picture was taken with my friends. I still have that photograph. It is the earliest one of me that exists. It shows a group of children, some smiling, others distracted by something beyond the camera. We are lined up in front of the hotel entrance; I am in the centre of the group and the two children on either side of me have their arms about my shoulders. I look happy and proud. There is nothing here of the special circumstances in which we found one another and which were reflected in our activities together. The picture looks very much like any school photograph.

III

OUR VISA, WHEN it was finally granted, was not what we had hoped for. Instead of an immigrant visa we received permission to visit the United States as tourists for a period of three months.

Tourist visas, ridiculous as they might seem under the circumstances, were not rare. The government used them as a way of preventing immigrants from taking their belongings with them. Everyone knew, of course, that once out of Poland these "tourists" would never return, but in the meantime the authorities had a pretext for keeping people's belongings until their safe return.

Our case was treated in the same way. We were informed of the sum of money we could take out of the country and we were instructed to deposit our few possessions with the police. There was no great financial loss, but there were attachments painful to break. My mother and my aunt had recovered a few objects from their parents' home and these they considered their last tangible link with the past. When they were forced to cut it, something in them changed forever. From then on they were unable to care where or how they lived. When they had the choice, they preferred anonymous, simple rooms, bare except for such items as were absolutely essential.

Some years later we were living in Montreal and I was old enough to notice the difference between our home and the homes of my friends. My family by this time could have afforded to live as they chose, but our rooms remained as bare as when we'd first arrived. When I reproached them with their indifference to the things I had suddenly discovered as important, they would look at me with an expression of pity that drove me to excesses of rage.

"My poor child," my aunt would begin, "if only you had known your grandfather's house, then you would see how ugly, how ridiculous, the houses of your friends are. Surely you don't expect us to imitate them."

Then, as if to compensate me for my loss, my aunt or my mother would search through their memories and come up with a few precious details: the hand-carved furniture my grandfather bought on his wedding trip to Italy; the richly coloured oriental rugs centred on lustrous floors; the huge marble bathtub, also Italian, where my mother and her sisters would have their bath, and the special rack that kept their towels warm for them.

"You cannot imagine," they would say to me, "what a feeling of beauty and elegance one had in those rooms. Every object was chosen for its own value and for its harmony with the rest of the house. We children took it all for granted, of course, but imagine how startled the Germans were when they burst into the house. They could never have imagined they would find anything like it in a small provincial Polish town."

Their reminiscences overshadowed every place we lived in. I was never able to persuade them to take any interest in acquiring objects I considered essential at that time, or to show any enthusiasm for my desperate efforts at embellishing our successive dwellings.

We left Warsaw by train for Gdynia, where we would take a boat for New York. The new friends we were leaving behind entrusted us with messages and pleas to their relatives in the new world. We said good-bye with mixed feelings of hope and regret.

In Gdynia we had a few hours before the boat sailed. We walked around aimlessly for a while. My mother stopped ahead of us in front of a hairdresser's shop. I paused to see what she was looking at. The place was empty of customers. Inside, beside strange machines stood two young, bored looking women. They seemed unaware of our presence as they patted their tightly curled hair and examined their dark red lips in small hand-mirrors. I thought they were very beautiful.

Suddenly my mother turned to my aunt. "Come on, we're going to have our hair cut." I followed them inside, thrilled and shy. For the next two hours I watched in fascination as the two young women worked over my aunt and my mother. Their long braids were loosened — my aunt's gold with white streaks, my mother's still all dark — and then cut. Finally, when it was all over, my mother and my aunt left the shop with hairdos very similar to those of the two beauticians. I liked the styles less on my mother and my aunt. Their new appearance made me uneasy for some time. It seemed to me they had acquired disguises in preparation for their new life.

My last memory of Poland was my first sight of the sea. On the day we sailed, the sky and the sea were dark and grey. The boat seemed smaller than I had expected. Before we were allowed to embark we had to submit to a very thorough search by the immigration officials. They kept us for over an hour, stripped us, and searched us with great care. When they did not find any hidden money or jewels, they contented themselves with removing my mother's watch, the last memento she had of my father.

This final gesture, and the humiliation of the search, must have made it easier for her to watch the coastline of her native land recede as the ship moved farther and farther from it. She never returned.

I stood next to my mother at the rail, understanding very little of what she was feeling or thinking. I wanted to go inside, to get away from the greyness, to see our cabins, but she held my hand tightly. I stayed with her until the coastline disappeared in fog and cloud.

Years later when I thought of that last vigil she had made me share with her, it occurred to me how similar it was to the watch at a graveside, when one doesn't turn one's back on the coffin until it is lowered out of sight. When there was nothing but sea and sky around us, my mother turned away and we went inside.

IV

MY UNCLE PERMITTED himself one last extravagance. Since we could not take any money out of the country he used all our available cash to book two first-class cabins for our passage to New York.

We sailed at the end of April. The sky remained grey and the sea turbulent. Most people suffered from seasickness. My mother, my aunt and my uncle lay weak and pale in their luxurious cabins, turning their heads away from the delicacies their steward brought them.

I, like most of the children, seemed to be unaffected by the heaving and swaying of the ship. While my family remained confined to their cabins, I was free to roam the vessel and do as I liked. The ship reminded me of the Hotel Bristol and I immediately felt at home on it. Here too there were companions approximately my age, with whom I could play games and explore the world where we would be confined for the next two weeks.

The *Batory*, a Polish liner, carried traces of its monthly contact with America. Naturally, it was these reflections of the civilization we were headed for that fascinated me. North America became the sum of these new experiences. For the first time in my life I saw a black man, tasted bananas and other strange foods, saw people swimming in a pool, listened to jazz, and discovered comic books and films.

Among the adults who were not seasick, there was one man who seemed to enjoy spending some time every day with us children. His name was Max, and he was an American citizen who had returned to his birthplace in Poland for a pre-war visit, to find himself trapped there by the war. Now, ten years later, he was making his return voyage to his home in Chicago.

Max first joined us one morning in the ship's library. We were leafing through old copies of American magazines, making wild comments to ourselves about the pictures and the people. Often their meaning was entirely lost on us and we laughed, like the young savages we were, at their apparent absurdity. Max seemed more interested in us than in the newspaper he was reading, and after a while he came over to find out why we were laughing. We showed him the mysterious photographs we found so amusing and Max explained their meaning. From then on he became our tutor and guide to the new world.

When we had exhausted the magazines, Max entertained us with stories of our new homeland. In particular, we liked his stories about Chicago and his life there when he had first arrived. Like all good storytellers he was not constricted by reality, and the details

he invented or rearranged ended in a picture of
Chicago that held us spellbound for hours.

Somehow he left us with the impression that all
Americans were physical giants. No people in Europe
could match them in height and weight, we were told.
Their feet and heads, in particular, were so large that
when old clothes from America arrived in Poland,
the hats and shoes would never fit the Poles and were
kept instead as objects of wonder and amazement.
I had read *Gulliver's Travels* that year in Polish, and
Max's stories of America's giants seemed to me entirely
plausible.

His stories were usually mixed with practical lessons.
He had taken it upon himself to teach us some facts
about our new home. For a start, we were greatly
impressed to learn that there were never any queues
in America. Incredible as it might seem, Max assured
us, there were enough goods to keep the stores constantly stocked. They never ran short.

Another feature of American life he promised we
would all enjoy was the plumbing. Max described this
with such care that his own appreciation of this great
invention was deeply impressed on us. We followed
every detail of his explanation and speculated among
ourselves about this marvellous mechanism which
flushed clean water, at will, as if by magic.

Max's talent lay in turning everything he talked
about into something extraordinary. In the beginning
I had timidly interrupted him to say I had seen a
gadget in the Hotel Bristol similar to the one he described. I was treated to a withering look of scorn.
Then he continued as if he hadn't heard me. At the
end I agreed with him. Nothing I had ever experienced was like the marvellous objects in Max's stories.

From the toilet we moved to the telephone. Again, I had seen one in the lobby of the Hotel Bristol, but it was an insignificant instrument compared to the magic boxes Max described. For hours he held us enthralled as he described how they worked. Every home in America, we were told, possessed this invention. Sometimes there was more than one in a house. Max decided it was essential for us to learn to use the telephone. We gathered around him and he began his lesson by making a drawing of a telephone, complete with every detail: dial face, letters, numbers. Next, each one of us was given an exchange and number by which we could demonstrate our proficiency with the telephone.

I remember dashing into my mother's cabin after one of these lessons, eager to impress her with my new sophistication. My mother was as unpredictable as always. My story set her off into a long laughing spell, and weak as she was in her seasickness, she could not stop. Finally, when she had regained her control, she pulled me over to her. Patting my hair gently and fighting to control the laughter that surged just beneath her words, she explained to me that she was quite familiar with the object I described. My grandfather had been one of the first people in Dobryd to have a telephone installed, and she and my father had also had one.

My mother's information robbed the telephone of some of its marvellous qualities; it was more commonplace than I had thought. Still, it seemed to me quite remarkable that we would live in a house where such a machine would exist totally at our disposal.

On the thirteenth day out we were told that we would shortly see the North American coastline. Along with this promise, the weather changed for the better. The sun shone steadily and the sea grew calm. Everyone on board recovered quickly. The next day, when the *Batory* sailed under Brooklyn Bridge and headed for its midtown dock, all the passengers were out on deck, lining the railings of the boat. Feelings of emotion and excitement were very intense. People ran about, laughed, clapped each other on the back, lifted up their children for a better view of the New York sky-line. Members of the ship's band came out on the deck with their instruments and they entertained us with rousing marching songs. We were all dizzy with the sun and the excitement of the moment.

When the boat docked we remained on board and waited for the customs officials. Some minutes later we were instructed to line up in front of desks set up by immigration officers and there to wait our turn to be processed. I found this delay particularly disappointing. Hadn't Max told us that there would be no more queues?

Fortunately, our wait was not long. Our turn came, our papers were stamped, and a young man wished us a pleasant stay. We were on our own.

We entered the passenger shed lost and confused. All around us people were embracing with obvious emotion. I knew that there was no one to meet us, but suddenly I wished desperately that one of these strangers would come though the crowd towards us and claim us.

I watched our fellow passengers leave with their baggage, presumably for new homes. Our journey, however, was not over. We were going on to Canada by train. My family had decided that their chances for political asylum were more favourable in Canada than in the United States.

We boarded the train for Montreal a few hours later. The amazing landscape of New York soon gave way to small towns of neat, compact houses. When night came we were out in the open countryside. Fields, hills, forests, train stations flashed by. There were few houses. As we moved farther north the land became more and more deserted. I looked in wonder at the lush views and the vast emptiness that seemed endless.

In the early morning hours we crossed the border into Canada. The countryside remained unchanged but a new feeling overcame me. I knew we were close to Montreal. The scenes outside my window mattered in a special way. Somewhere, in the midst of them I would begin a new life.